The Infancy Narratives

STUDIES IN THE SYNOPTIC GOSPELS

by Herman Hendrickx, CICM

The Infancy Narratives
The Passion Narratives of the Synoptic Gospels
The Resurrection Narratives of the Synoptic Gospels
The Sermon on the Mount

The Infancy Narratives

Herman Hendrickx

Geoffrey Chapman
London

A Geoffrey Chapman book published by
Cassell Ltd
1 Vincent Square, London SW1P 2PN

First edition copyright 1975 by East Asian Pastoral Institute, PO Box 1815,
Manila, Philippines
Revised edition © Geoffrey Chapman, a division of Cassell Ltd. 1984

Cum permissu superiorum

This edition first published 1984

ISBN 0 225 66398 8

British Library Cataloguing in Publication Data

Hendrickx, Herman
    The infancy narratives.—Rev. ed.— (Studies in the synoptic gospels)
    1. Jesus Christ—Childhood 2. Bible. N.T. Matthew—Commentaries 3. Bible N.T.
Luke—Commentaries
    I. Title II. Series
    232.9'2   BT310

Typeset in VIP Times by
D. P. Media Limited, Hitchin, Hertfordshire

Printed and bound in Great Britain by Biddles Limited, Guildford

Contents

Preface

This book had its beginnings in a series of lectures on the Infancy Narratives given to theology students and catechists in Manila.

Although it is generally accepted that the first two chapters of Matthew and Luke did not form part of the earliest Christian preaching, they do occupy a special place in New Testament literature. Biblical scholars have done a great deal to reveal the significance of these narratives and it is to make the fruits of their labours available to a wider public that I have written this book.

The book is organized as a commentary on the texts followed by a final chapter about preaching on the infancy gospels. It is impossible to account in detail for every idea or formulation for which I am indebted to New Testament scholarship and such an apparatus would be beyond the scope and format of this publication. Notes have therefore been kept to a minimum but a full bibliography is included, together with suggestions for further reading. I am deeply indebted to the work of many biblical scholars and I wish to record here my appreciation and thanks.

I would also like to thank all those who encouraged me at any stage of this work. I am especially indebted to Rev. John Reilly, SJ, of the East Asian Pastoral Institute, for invaluable help in the preparation of the manuscript for publication, and to Rev. Martin Ramsauer, SJ, Publications Manager in the East Asian Pastoral Institute, whose meticulous care and concern were so obvious at all times.

Note to the Revised Edition

The first edition of this book was published at the beginning of 1975 and with a few exceptions could take into account only the literature on the Infancy Narratives published until 1973. Ten years have passed during which a considerable number of monograph studies and periodical articles were published.

Therefore the author and the publisher, Geoffrey Chapman, decided to update the bibliography for this revised edition, and to revise the book in the light of some important recent publications, especially George M. Soares Prabhu, *The Formula Quotations in the Infancy Narrative of Matthew* (1976), Raymond E. Brown, *The Birth of the Messiah* (1977), and Lucien Legrand, *L'Annonce à Marie* (1981). We trust that this revision will make the book even more readable and useful for the reading public we have in mind.

I would like to express here my gratitude to Miss Anne Boyd, Chief Editor, without whose interest this second edition would not have been possible, and Miss Fiona McKenzie, Senior House Editor, for her invaluable editorial work.

1   The Infancy Narratives

The earliest preaching

The stories about Jesus' birth and childhood were not part of the earliest Christian preaching. A very simple and obvious indication of this is their absence from the gospels of Mark and John. Mark's introductory verse, 'The beginning of the gospel of Jesus Christ, the Son of God', is immediately followed by the preaching of John the Baptist and corresponds to Mt 3 and Lk 3. The reason why the infancy narratives were not part of the earliest Christian preaching becomes clear when we understand the meaning of the term *gospel*.

Although for many people the term *gospel* might suggest primarily the four gospels, its usual meaning in the New Testament is the good news of the divine redemption made manifest in Jesus and introducing the new era. Originally, *gospel* meant the living, spoken word of preaching. In fact, the written gospels appeared only after several decades of a spoken gospel. If the oldest gospels are to be regarded as the written record of the verbal preaching of the early Church, it is worth while considering what they spoke about.

An outline of this preaching may be found in the speeches of the first part of the Acts of the Apostles (see Acts 2:22–39; 3:12–26; 4:8–12; 5:30–32; 10:36–43). In these passages the apostles speak as witnesses of the realities which they themselves have seen, heard and experienced. The central truth which they proclaim is Jesus' resurrection from the dead and his exaltation. Peter concludes his sermon on the day of Pentecost: 'Let all the house of Israel therefore know assuredly that God has made him both Lord and Christ, this Jesus whom you crucified' (Acts 2:36). This forms the central piece of evidence. To this were added the accounts of the finding of the empty tomb, the arrest, trial and crucifixion of Jesus, which were partly intended for the instruction of the community.

Gradually, the public ministry of Jesus (teaching and miracles) also found a place in this instruction: 'You know the word which he sent to Israel, preaching good news of peace by Jesus Christ (he is Lord of all), the word which was proclaimed throughout all Judea, beginning from Galilee after the baptism which John preached: how God anointed Jesus of Nazareth with the Holy Spirit and with power; how he went about doing good and healing all that were oppressed by the devil, for God was with him' (Acts 10:36–38).

The references to Jesus's life were never to events earlier than the activity of John the Baptist and Jesus' baptism in the river Jordan. We find no mention in these ancient outline sketches of what preceded Jesus' public ministry. The preaching makes frequent reference to Jesus' descent from David (see Acts 2:30; 13:23; Rom 1:3), and Luke says that 'when Jesus began his ministry, he was about thirty years of age' (Lk 3:23), but there is no mention anywhere of his birth at Bethlehem and the years at Nazareth.

All this seems easy to explain, since the apostles were not first-hand eyewitnesses of what happened in the first period of Jesus' life, and the earliest preaching was not interested in Jesus' human family circumstances. Moreover, the traditions about Jesus' hidden life were not confirmed by the public's knowledge of them, as a large number of the reports about his public life were.

In short, the infancy narratives occupy a special place in the New Testament literature. They do not belong to the core of the gospel proper. They may be Matthew's and Luke's answer to a growing interest in the person of Jesus which eventually extended, beyond the beginning of Jesus' public ministry, into the earlier years of his hidden life. The primitive preaching focused first of all on Jesus' death and resurrection and, a little later, on his public ministry. It was only considerably later, though still within the apostolic period, that interest developed in Jesus' early years in Nazareth and his birth in Bethlehem. This was answered by Matthew and Luke, though not in the form of a chronicle of incidents of Jesus' birth and youth.

Matthew and Luke

Of the four evangelists only Matthew and Luke describe the infancy of Jesus. Yet there are striking differences in the approach of each. A brief comparison of Mt 1 – 2 and Lk 1 – 2 will show this. While doing this, however, we should not assume, consciously or unconsciously, that the two authors, Matthew and Luke, are each attempting, in their own way, to give an accurate account of the birth of Jesus. Their intentions could be different, and therefore we should resist any inclination to harmonize the two accounts.

We can discern five important differences.

(1)   In Matthew, the genealogy comes first and runs from *Abraham* to *Jesus* called Christ. It is adapted, leaving out, for example, three of the kings mentioned in the Old Testament (Ahaziah, Joash, and Amaziah), and with obviously too few generations in its third pattern of fourteen (see Mt 1:17). It always follows the *ruling* Davidic line. Its

most distinctive figure, however, is the mention of four women: *Tamar*, *Rahab*, *Ruth* and *the wife of Uriah* (*Bathsheba*). In Luke, the genealogy has no relation to the infancy narrative. It follows the baptism of Jesus and is connected with the phrase *beloved Son* pronounced at the baptism (Lk 3:22). The genealogy runs in the opposite direction, from *Jesus* by a chain of simple genitives all the way to *the son of Adam, the son of God* (Lk 3:23–38). The line of David goes via Nathan, i.e., a *non-ruling* line of the Davidic family. The Davidic element is not stressed; the point clearly is: *son of God*.

(2)   In Matthew, *Joseph* is the most important character. He receives the revelation and through him the action progresses. Dreams are vehicles of revelation, a phenomenon peculiar to Matthew. The Greek phrase *kat' onar*, 'in a dream', is found five times in Mt 1 – 2 and also in Mt 27:19, referring to the dream of Pilate's wife; but nowhere else in the New Testament. In Luke, *Mary* is the recipient of revelation and Joseph merely stands by.

(3)   None of the events mentioned in Mt 2 is mentioned or alluded to in Lk 1 – 2: the visit of the Magi, the flight into Egypt, the massacre of the innocents, the return from Egypt and the continued flight to Galilee and Nazareth. On the other hand, the story of John the Baptist, which occupies almost half of Luke's infancy narrative, is not even mentioned in Mt 1 – 2; the same is true of the visit to Elizabeth, the presentation of Jesus in the Temple, the finding of Jesus in the Temple, and the three hymns, the *Magnificat* of Mary, the *Benedictus* of Zechariah, and the *Nunc Dimittis* of Simeon.

(4)   Both evangelists mention *Bethlehem* and *Nazareth*, but in different ways. According to Matthew, Joseph and Mary live in Bethlehem and their settling in Nazareth is due to a special guidance at a latter time, after the flight into and return from Egypt. According to Luke, Joseph and Mary live in Nazareth, they go to Bethlehem for the specific purpose of the census, and they return to their town after the presentation in the Temple. In Luke, there is no evil Herod in the background, only shepherds and pious Jews, Simeon and Anna. In Luke too we have the elaborate parallelism between John the Baptist and Jesus.

(5)   In Matthew, the text rests on *formula quotations* or *fulfilment quotations*. These are quotations from the Old Testament introduced by a phrase like 'to fulfil what was spoken by the prophet'. There is one such quotation for almost each point in Matthew's account. There are no such quotations in Luke, where the relation to the Old Testament is expressed rather in subtle allusions, which are concentrated in the hymns and canticles.

These differences are more drastic than anywhere else in the canonical gospels, even if we compare the Synoptics with the Fourth Gospel. They should caution us against treating Mt 1 – 2 and Lk 1 – 2 as alternative birth narratives. As Raymond Brown has said,

> . . . our problems deepen when we compare the two Infancy Narratives, one to the other; for, despite ingenious attempts at harmonization, the basic stories are virtually irreconcilable (cf. Matt 2:14 and Luke 2:39). They agree in so few details that . . . they cannot both be historical *in toto*.[1]

However, in spite of these very important differences, there are in the narratives of Matthew and Luke some very interesting agreements:

(1) Mary is the mother of Jesus; Joseph is considered to be the father of Jesus (Mt 1:21, 25; Lk 2:16, 41, 48).
(2) The miraculous virginal conception (Mt 1:18–25; Lk 1:26–38).
(3) Joseph is only the legal father (Mt 1:16, 20; Lk 1:35).
(4) The birth of Jesus at Bethlehem in Judea (Mt 2:1, 5f.; Lk 2:4–6, 11, 15).
(5) Born during the days of Herod (Mt 2:1; Lk 1:5).
(6) The name Jesus communicated by an angel (Mt 1:21 to Joseph; Lk 1:31 to Mary).
(7) Jesus belongs to the family of David (Mt 1:1ff.; Lk 1:32).
(8) Jesus spends his youth in Nazareth (Mt 2:23 from the time of the return from Egypt; Lk 2:39 immediately after the presentation in the Temple).

Such agreements between two independent narratives that otherwise differ so drastically, and which are, therefore, not intentional, may indicate historical fact. Many scholars accept that in the infancy narratives we are in possession of certain basic historical facts.

Midrash

In recent years the term *midrash* has been found increasingly often in studies of the literary forms of the New Testament, especially those of the infancy narratives of Matthew and Luke. To the uninitiated reader it is not clear what this term means. In fact, the terminology is far from clear, and biblical scholars warn us about the *elasticity* of the word. Although it has become clear that too narrow a definition can be as misleading as a vague one, some clarification is certainly needed. What do authors mean when they say a passage of Scripture is *midrash*?

Among many ways of describing the meaning of *midrash* we give here one attempt by a recognized biblical scholar to elaborate a definition of *midrash* and to list its most important characteristics:

. . . rabbinic *midrash* is a literature concerned with the Bible; it is a literature about a literature. A *midrash* is a work that attempts to make a text of Scripture understandable, useful, and relevant for a later generation. It is the text of Scripture which is the point of departure, and it is for the sake of the text that the *midrash* exists. The treatment of any given text may be creative or non-creative, but the literature as a whole is predominantly creative in its handling of the biblical material. The interpretation is accomplished sometimes by rewriting the biblical material, sometimes by commenting upon it. In either case the *midrash* may go as far afield as it wishes provided that at some stage at least there is to be found some connection, implicit or explicit, between the biblical text and the new midrashic composition. At times this connection with the text may be convincing, at times it may be desperate; it is sufficient merely that a connection be there. Frequently the midrashic literature is characterized by a careful analysis of and attention to the biblical text.[2]

Most specialists in Jewish literature have also stressed that it is not easy to define the complex phenomenon which is usually referred to as *midrash*. One of them writes:

Midrash is in effect a whole world which can be discovered only by accepting its complexity at the outset. It is pervasive throughout the whole Jewish approach to the Bible, which could in its entirety be called *midrash*. Technique and method cannot be separated, even if they lead to different literary genres. Midrash may be described but not *defined*, for it is also a way of thinking and reasoning which is often disconcerting to us.[3]

In a simple way, then, what can we say of *midrash*? Literally this term means 'research', and indicates a distinctively Jewish literary form. It is a composition that explains the scriptures and seeks to make them understandable and meaningful for a later generation. Its aim is very practical: the author wants to set forth the contemporary value and significance of older texts. Two of the most characteristic features frequently found in a *midrash* are: (1) a careful attention to the details of the biblical narrative and a desire to explain the reasons for happenings and draw out applications for the present; (2) the biblical material is handled creatively: details are changed to fit the purposes of the author and events are idealized and even embellished with legendary material to make them fuller, more vivid and edifying.

The midrashic commentaries on the scriptures originated, it seems, from two sources: the exegesis given in the schools of the rabbis in response to a variety of questions prompted by the text; and the homilies in the synagogues, which looked to the edification of those present. Two types of *midrash* are, therefore, distinguished, the *halachah* (conduct, literally 'walking'), and the *haggadah* (narrative). The *halachah* is an explanation of the law, deriving principles, laws and rules of conduct for the contemporary situation; the *haggadah* is an explanation of the narrative passages of the Pentateuch with an extremely wide range of edifying lessons for the actual present.

Midrash looks for edifying lessons; it is a meditation on the sacred text or an imaginative reconstruction of the scene or episode narrated. Its aim is always the practical application to the present; thus a law may be restated or a narrative retold not in terms of its own historical context, but in such a way that it gives light and direction to the generation which writes the *midrash*.

The pericope of the death of Judas (Mt 27:3–10) is a good example of a New Testament *midrash*. The context shows that the incident cannot possibly have taken place at the stage where it is inserted into the events by Matthew. The chief priests and elders, for instance, cannot be in the Temple, since they are on their way to Pilate! Also, the description of Judas' death is very different from that found in Acts (1:16–20). The pericope is a subtle composition built up with Old Testament allusions and passages. Judas is said to have hanged himself in circumstances which recall the story of Ahithophel who, having betrayed his friend and king David and seeing that his plans were not going to work out as he had hoped, 'went off home . . . and hanged himself' (II Sam 17:23). The thirty silver pieces and the treasury remind us of the prophet Zechariah who was appointed by God as the *shepherd of Israel*, but who wanted to resign because of the people's stubbornness and asked them to pay him his wages. They paid him *thirty silver pieces* to get rid of him. Then God said: 'Cast them in the treasury' (see Zech 11:4–14; especially 12–13). This text is combined with the idea of the *purchase of a field* suggested by Jer 32:6–15. Moreover, Jer 18:2f. and 19:1, 10–12 speak of *potters*.

All this may seem rather subtle, but we should not forget that one of the characteristics of *midrash* is precisely its subtlety! Summing up, we could say that Matthew's purpose is not to provide accurate information about the death of Judas. This would have very little salvific meaning. Rather, by means of a *midrash* combination of allusions and quotations, he wants to stress the *innocence* of Jesus. This is one of the most important aims of Matthew's passion narrative as a whole. One way he does this is by evaluating the trial as a fake trial (admitted by Judas and the Sanhedrin themselves, Mt 27:4–6), and comparing Judas' action to that of Ahithophel. In this light Jesus appears as the *new David*, or *son of David*. The price paid for Jesus was the price paid to get rid of the shepherd of Israel (Zechariah). Jesus, therefore, appears also as the *Shepherd of the people of God*, at present rejected but ultimately victorious. David and the shepherd figure are closely connected.

One characteristic of *midrash* which was pointed out earlier is that the *midrash*, or new composition, must exist *for the sake of the biblical text*. Does this imply that the Old Testament text is more important than the actual contemporary situation? A specialist in Jewish literature already quoted comments:

> It seems to us that this is the heart of the problem and that the tension between the two poles of midrash which assume a biblical *text* and its *adaptation* is clear. Is it primarily concerned with serving the text or with using the text to respond to the needs of actualization? Is the chief purpose to write a new composition in order to respond to actual circumstances (e.g., to the needs of the liturgy . . .), or does the text remain the center of interest and the ultimate reference? . . . Let us say only that the text is very often little more than a *stimulus* for a composition which is developed in complete independence of it. . . . It is above all for the benefit of the community that the contemporary meaning of the Word of God is sought. These considerations are essential for understanding the use of Scripture in the New Testament and what we could call *Christian midrash*. According to Wright (pp. 140f.) Matthew 1–2 cannot be called *midrash* because the citations 'seem to be used not to direct attention to the OT material, so that it might be explained, but to explain the person of Jesus'. This is an example of the 'Copernican revolution' which is effected by the fact that henceforth God 'has spoken to us by a Son', . . . (Heb 1:2) . . . Christ became the key to the Scriptures. . . . The 'inquiry' is henceforth centered on him. . . . But this radical change did not alter any – or hardly any – midrashic methods, and Paul in II Corinthians 3 makes a Christian midrash in the same manner as a Jewish rabbi.[4]

The Old Testament texts of Mt 1 – 2 are not used to explain the Old Testament but to describe the person of Jesus, and Lk 1 – 2 interprets the Christ-event by means of analogies from the Old Testament. In both gospels the writer's reflection on the new events is set forth in midrashic form. It seems to us, therefore, that the term *midrash* – or, if one prefers, *Christian midrash* – can be rightly used for the infancy narratives. It is the *meaning* of the birth and life of Jesus Christ for first-century Christians which clearly is the focus of the evangelists' attention. The Old Testament texts they employ or refer to in their infancy narratives are for them a stimulus and a means of achieving this purpose. In this sense the infancy narratives can be called *midrash*.

2 The Infancy Narrative of Matthew

The general structure

The first two chapters of Matthew's gospel, like the entire work, show unmistakable signs of being a well-constructed whole rather than a simple series of events strung together chronologically. Through their subtitles the Jerusalem Bible and most other Bible editions create the impression that Matthew's infancy narrative consists of a series of longer and shorter stories. But in the Greek New Testament there are no such subtitles, and here the introductory chapters of Matthew form a self-contained whole.

Mt 1:18 takes up Mt 1:16 and further develops what is said in this verse. In the same way Mt 2:1 takes up the final sentence of the previous scene, Mt 1:25. Thus the evangelist invites us to read the two chapters, from the genealogy (Mt 1:1–17), through the announcement of Joseph (Mt 1:18–25), to the appearance of the Magi and what follows until Jesus and his parents settle in Nazareth (Mt 2:1–23).

Prologue of Matthew

Some scholars hold that the prologue of Matthew extends from Mt 1:1 to Mt 4:16, for this section gives a preliminary understanding of Jesus which is necessary in order to evaluate properly his ministry, death and resurrection. The gospel itself contains indications of its structural divisions.

The beginnings of new sections are marked out by identical formulas. Mt 4:17 reads: 'From that time Jesus began to preach, saying, "Repent, for the kingdom of heaven is at hand"', and in Mt 16:21 we read: 'From that time Jesus began to show his disciples that he must go to Jerusalem and suffer many things . . .'. Now within Mt 1:1 – 4:16 there are certain marks of unity. The phrase 'in those days' (Mt 3:1) is a loose connective which links the birth narrative editorially with the account of John the Baptist, of Jesus' baptism and temptation. Furthermore, there are seven *formula* or *fulfilment quotations* in Mt 1:1 – 4:16, and seven is a favourite number to express completeness (see e.g., seven parables of the kingdom in Mt 13, whereas the Marcan source, Mk 4, has only four parables).

We could, perhaps, say that the *Book of Generation* embraces Mt 1:1 – 4:16 and has two themes: Mt 1 – 2 is concerned with the Messiah, the son of David; and Mt 3:1 – 4:16 deals with the real Israelite, the son of Abraham. Nevertheless we prefer the view of those who consider Mt 1 – 2 as an independent whole.

Looking now at the structure of Mt 1 – 2, we find that it consists of five or six pericopes, depending on whether we consider Mt 2:13–15 and Mt 2:16–18 as two separate pericopes or as only one:

(1)   the genealogy (Mt 1:1–17);
(2)   the announcement of Jesus' birth (Mt 1:18–25);
(3)   the visit of the Magi (Mt 2:1–12);
(4)   the flight into Egypt (Mt 2:13–15);
(5)   the massacre of the innocents (Mt 2:16–18);
(6)   the return from Egypt (Mt 2:19–23).

We have a genealogy and five (or four) episodes dealing with Jesus. Among these episodes, the visit of the Magi stands apart because it differs from the other passages in a number of characteristic features. Because of the similar grammatical structure at the beginning of three of these passages (Mt 1:20; 2:13; 2:19),[5] some would consider this recurring structure a literary device of Matthew's indicating among other things that the flight into Egypt and the massacre of the innocents are to be considered as a single pericope. There would then be three main divisions: the genealogy (Mt 1:1–17), the story of the Magi (Mt 2:1–12) and three *Joseph stories*, so called because Joseph has an important role in them; Mt 1:18–25; 2:13–18; 2:19–23.

The Joseph stories

These three Joseph stories have a number of common characteristics:

(1)   The introductory situation is grammatically similar:
      (a)   'But as he considered this' (Mt 1:20);
      (b)   'Now when they had departed' (Mt 2:13);
      (c)   'But when Herod died' (Mt 2:19).

(2)   The angel appears in a dream and brings the divine instruction:
      (a)   'behold, an angel of the Lord appeared to him in a dream, saying' (Mt 1:20);
      (b)   'behold, an angel of the Lord appeared to Joseph in a dream and said' (Mt 2:13);
      (c)   'behold, an angel of the Lord appeared in a dream to Joseph in Egypt, saying' (Mt 2:19).

(3)   Joseph hears the message and acts:
  (a)   'When Joseph woke from sleep, he did . . .' (Mt 1:24);
  (b)   'And he rose and took the child and his mother' (Mt 2:14);
  (c)   'And he rose and took the child and his mother' (Mt 2:21).

(4)   A scripture text is fulfilled:
  (a)   'All this took place to fulfil what the Lord had spoken by the prophet' (Mt 1:22);
  (b)   'This was to fulfil what the Lord had spoken by the prophet' (Mt 2:15);
  (c)   'That what was spoken by the prophets might be fulfilled' (Mt 2:23).

Each story shows a close parallelism between the instruction given by the angel and the execution by Joseph:

  (a)   'an angel . . . do not fear to take Mary your wife . . . and you shall call his name Jesus' (Mt 1:20–21);
        'When Joseph woke from sleep, he did as the angel of the Lord commanded him; he took his wife . . . and he called his name Jesus' (Mt 1:24–25);
  (b)   'an angel . . . Rise, take the child and his mother, and flee to Egypt, and remain there till I tell you' (Mt 2:13);
        'And he rose and took the child and his mother by night, and departed to Egypt, and remained there' (Mt 2:14);
  (c)   'an angel . . . Rise, take the child and his mother, and go to the land of Israel' (Mt 2:20);
        'And he rose and took the child and his mother, and went to the land of Israel' (Mt 2:21).

This feature undoubtedly suggests Joseph's total obedience to the divine guidance. This is probably intended to illustrate what is meant by Mt 1:19 saying that Joseph was a 'just man'. The parallelism of construction and vocabulary in these Joseph stories is obvious and, compared with these three stories, the visit of the Magi is seen to be very different.

Continuity

If we take Mt 1 – 2 as a whole, there are definite elements giving *continuity* among the pericopes. First of all, there is *Joseph*, the most important character after Jesus. He is found in four of the six episodes, or four of the five, if we consider the flight into Egypt and the massacre of the innocents as one pericope. In Mt 2 the continuity is also assured by *Herod* whose name is found in all the pericopes of that chapter.

Another form of continuity is the connection between the successive pericopes. They call for each other. Mt 1:18, 'Now the birth (*genesis*) of Jesus Christ took place in this way', recalls Mt 1:1, 'The book of the genealogy (*geneseōs*) of Jesus Christ'. The genealogy ends in Mt 1:16 with Joseph in an abnormal way; up to that point we find always: *N. was the father of N.* But now we do not find *Joseph was the father of Jesus*, but *and Jacob the father of Joseph the husband of Mary, of whom Jesus was born*. This anomaly raises the question of the exact relationship between Mary and Joseph and the exact nature of Joseph's fatherhood. Mt 1:18–25 answers this question: Jesus is really the son of Joseph and, therefore, a descendant of David. Because Joseph is the legal father of Jesus, who is conceived by Mary in a miraculous, virginal way, Joseph, son of David, gives him the name.

We have a slight hiatus between Mt 1 and 2, but there is also a connection. Mt 2:1, 'Now when Jesus was born (*gennēthentos*) in Bethlehem', explicitly makes the connection with Mt 1. The term 'born' (*gennēthentos*) echoes Mt 1:16, 'of whom Jesus was born' (*egennēthē*). But there is more than just a literary connection. Jesus is the Saviour of Israel, his people (Mt 1:21). How will this people receive him? This we find in Mt 2:1–12. Whereas the Magi react positively, his own people react with fear and murderous plans. These plans are the occasion of the flight (Mt 2:13–15). The execution of the murderous plans follows (Mt 2:16–18). The danger once averted, the return is as expected (Mt 2:19–23).

Old Testament quotations

After the genealogical introduction, the author divides his material into five (four) parts. Finding Old Testament passages which are fulfilled by the events of Jesus' earthly life, he uses these biblical texts with some freedom, but not without purpose. The purpose of these quotations is clear: they are quoted to show that Jesus fulfils the will of God as expressed in the Old Testament scriptures and hence is the Messiah. Four of these quotations, those found in the Joseph stories, are introduced by a typically Matthean formula 'to fulfil what was spoken by the prophet' (with slight variations; Mt 1:22; 2:15, 17, 23). This formula every time directs the whole story toward the quotations, which are really the core of the pericopes, and are called *fulfilment quotations*. The stories appear, as it were, in the shadow of the quotations. We get only very concise, schematic, sometimes even colourless sketches of facts without any details of time, place and persons, so that many questions remain unanswered.

The fulfilment or formula quotations are characterized by three distinctive common features. Firstly, a typical fulfilment formula, whose most characteristic word is the passive of the verb 'to fulfil'. Secondly, the quotations have a commentary function; they are 'asides' of the evangelist rather than part of his narrative. Thirdly (not easy to discern in English translation), they have a mixed text form, closer to the Hebrew than the other Old Testament quotations in the gospels, which tend to follow the Septuagint Greek text.

We should note that the quotation in the story of the Magi (Mt 2:1–12; specifically Mt 2:5–6) differs from the other quotations. This quotation is not introduced by the fulfilment formula but is part of the story itself and is put in the mouth of the 'chief priests and the scribes of the people'. This kind of quotation is called a *contextual quotation*, because it belongs to the context of the story. In that sense it differs basically from the *fulfilment quotation* which does not really belong to the context of the story and, as it were, interrupts the progression.

This free but meaningful use of the Old Testament, along with the built-in balance which the author achieves throughout the narrative, makes it clear that the events of Jesus' infancy were set down here, not simply because they happened, but primarily because they could be used to bring out Matthew's didactic and apologetic purposes.

An extensive examination of the structure and theme of Mt 1 – 2 leads to the conclusion that these chapters consist of two parts which in content and structure form two closed, though interconnected, units. Jesus' Messiahship is demonstrated from his origins (Mt 1) and from the child's destiny (Mt 2). The emphasis in Mt 2 is placed upon the significance of the Messiahship: the messianic prophecies are fulfilled through the repetition of the childhood destiny of Jacob-Israel and Moses, typologically understood.

Geographical names

Mt 2 is dominated by geographical names. This is a striking contrast to Mt 1, which does not contain a single geographical name, not even where we would expect it (e.g. in Mt 1:18). Mt 2 begins with the mention of *Bethlehem of Judea*, it takes us to *Egypt*, describes the massacre at *Bethlehem*, takes us out of *Egypt* back to the land of *Israel*, bypasses *Judea*, takes us into *Galilee* and settles down in *Nazareth*. For Matthew the *itinerary* is not a frame secondary to his intention. On the contrary, these geographical names constitute what really matters, as can be seen from his use of the *formula* or *fulfilment quotations*: the common denominator for the quotations in Mt 2 is the geographical names. These mark the stages reached in the itinerary.

At two points it becomes obvious that the quotations have the *locations* rather than the events as their focus. First, the prophecy 'Out of Egypt have I called my son' (Mt 2:15) is placed by Matthew, not where the call out of Egypt takes place (Mt 2:19), but where the word 'Egypt' occurs for the first time (Mt 2:13–15). Hence it is obvious that Matthew wants to emphasize *Egypt* in the itinerary. Secondly, several of the original Greek manuscripts and the Targum[6] suppress the name *Ramah* by translating 'in the highland' (*en tēi hupsēlēi*). This may well have been the prevailing interpretation in Judaism, and hence Matthew's use of the geographical name is not self-evident (it goes against the almost general interpretation of the text in his time). The name *Ramah* is used in order to serve the geographical interest of the quotation.

If the geographical names are what give the structure to Mt 2, then this chapter gives the answer to a question similar to the two raised in Jn 7:41–42: 'Is the Christ to come from Galilee? Has not the scripture said that the Christ is descended from David, and comes from Bethlehem, the village where David was?' In the Fourth Gospel these questions are left open. Is this a literary device or evidence of the author's lack of knowledge or lack of interest in any Bethlehem tradition? In this connection it is significant that this is the only passage in the Fourth Gospel where the name of David is mentioned. In this gospel Jesus is never called *son of David*, and it is solemnly stated, 'My kingship is not of this world' (Jn 18:36). But the question is a real one: how was it that Jesus the Messiah came from a Galilean village? Hence the whole of Mt 2 has its climax in the last verse: 'He shall be called a Nazarene' (Mt 2:23). The chapter shows how God himself, according to prophecies and through divine and angelic intervention, leads Joseph, and thereby Jesus, from Bethlehem to Nazareth. The title that could well be written over Mt 2 might be: How it came to pass that the Messiah came from Nazareth.

Personal names

Once it has been recognized how Mt 2 is focused on the geographical names, it is clear that Mt 1 has not only a similar apologetic purpose, but also a similar structure, now centred on personal names. 'And he called his name Jesus' (Mt 1:25) corresponds to 'He shall be called a Nazarene' (Mt 2:23), and the geographical name *Nazareth* implied in *Nazarene*. We have already mentioned the striking absence of any geographical names in Mt 1. Of greater significance is that *from the point of view of literary form*, Mt 1:18–25 could be called a legend of divine name-giving, with its Matthean point in the last words, 'and he called his name Jesus'.

Most commentators on Mt 1 – 2 draw a decisive line of demarcation between the genealogy (Mt 1:1–17) and the Matthean birth narrative (Mt 1:18 – 2:23). But it should be recognized that the whole of Mt 1 has its own integrity and that the line of demarcation really lies between Mt 1 and Mt 2. The genealogy in its Matthean form points to what follows in Mt 1:18–25 by its accentuation of the Davidic line. This is clear from the way in which David is stressed in Mt 1:1, 17, possibly also from the formula *three times fourteen* (see below); and in Mt 1:6

NB the royal status of David, and only of David, is stressed. Whereas the whole series of names refers to kings of Israel, only David is referred to as *David the king*. Δαυιδ τον βασιλεα

We may conclude, therefore, that Matthew's infancy narrative concentrates on the important personal names (chapter 1) and the geographical indications (chapter 2) of the messianic event. Mt 3:1ff. joins Mk 1:1ff. in relating the preaching of John the Baptist and the baptism of Jesus. If Matthew thought of his infancy narrative as an account of events, the phrase 'in those days' (Mt 3:1) would seem rather strange and give evidence of a carelessness we do not normally find in Matthew's handling of his sources. If, however, our interpretation of Matthew's infancy narrative is correct, then Mt 3:1 is easily understood, because here, and only here, begins the account of the actual events. This account is preceded in Mt 1 – 2 by an answer to the question *Who* the Messiah is and *From where* he comes. To remain really faithful to Matthew's intention we should not call this a *birth narrative*.

In order clearly and systematically to summarize this explanation, we give a schematic presentation of the first two chapters of Matthew:

Outline of Matthew's infancy narrative

1:1–17	genealogy		
1:18–25	announcement of birth	Isa 7:14	(1:23)
2:1–12	visit of the Magi	Mic 5:2(1)	(2:6) Bethlehem
2:13–15	flight into Egypt	Hos 11:1	(2:15) Egypt
2:16–18	massacre of the innocents	Jer 31:15	(2:18) Ramah
2:19–23	return from Egypt	?	(2:23) Nazareth (Nazarene)

In the third column we give the Old Testament text quoted in each pericope. Mic 5:2 (5:1 in the Hebrew text) is different in character. In the fourth column we give the passage in Matthew where the quotation is found and the place name mentioned in the quotation.

The various motifs

To perceive the full meaning of any piece of writing the reader must first recognize what literary form its author employed. Since the aim of a biblical scholar today is to find the theological content of the inspired writings of sacred scripture, his point of departure must be the literary structures that the sacred writer used. When we examine the first two chapters of Matthew we are led to suspect that they involve a more complex literary device than a simple, objective description of facts. But before forming a comprehensive view of the character of the work, an analysis of the *various motifs* is required.

Today, unlike some years ago, it is widely admitted that the literary motifs of Matthew's infancy narrative are inspired by Hebrew rather than pagan sources. The main motifs are:

(1)   Davidic origin of Jesus;
(2)   previous announcements in dreams;
(3)   slaughter of the innocents:
(4)   the star of the Magi;
(5)   the flight into Egypt;
(6)   the return to Bethlehem, later to Nazareth.

Davidic origin of Jesus

Matthew's account begins with the genealogy, by which he established that *Jesus was descended from King David*. This is established in three ways: (a) by the genealogy itself, (b) by explicit testimonies in the infancy account, and (c) by the fact that Jesus was born in Bethlehem. Matthew's apologetic intent in presenting his genealogy is clear from the opening line: 'The book of the genealogy of Jesus Christ, the son of David, the son of Abraham' (Mt 1:1). Matthew attempts to establish the Davidic ancestry of Jesus by his genealogy and explicit testimonies. The angel calls Joseph 'son of David' (Mt 1:20), and as such he has to give the child its name, thus accepting the legal fatherhood of the child and making it a 'son of David'. The chief priests and scribes know of the prophecy of Micah which said that the Messiah would be *born in Bethlehem*.

Previous announcements in dreams

The second motif we discover in the infancy narrative is the *pre-announcement in dreams* of the hero's birth and mission. Three times in the infancy narrative an angel appears to Joseph in a dream: (a) to announce the virginal conception (Mt 1:20), (b) to order the flight into Egypt (Mt 2:13), and (c) to command the family's return to the land of Israel (Mt 2:19). Some commentators underline the parallel between Matthew's announcement of the birth by means of a dream and the midrashic legends concerning the birth of Moses. The Book of Exodus does not mention any previous announcement of the birth of Moses. But the legend that grew up around Moses is prolific in dreams announcing his birth.

Various legends say that his father Amram, his sister Miriam, and even Pharaoh himself dreamed of Moses' birth. We read in one such legend[7] that the spirit of the Lord came over Miriam, and she had a dream in the night. Later she related to her parents what the dream figure dressed in red had said: 'Tell your father and your mother that he who will be born to them during the night will be carried away and thrown into the water, and that for him the water will be bisected. And signs and prodigies will be brought to pass through him. He will save my people of Israel and he will be its guide.' Note the similarity of this last sentence and Mt 1:21: 'and you shall call his name Jesus, for he will save his people', also announced in a dream.

The three dreams of the infancy narrative involve Joseph. Since very little seems to have been known about him (he never appears in the stories of Jesus' ministry), his picture may very well have been fleshed out with items borrowed from the stories about the patriarch Joseph. Indeed, the latter is described as a 'man of dreams' or 'specialist in dreams' (Gen 37:19; RSV's 'dreamer' is a rather weak translation). Moreover, the patriarch Joseph went down to Egypt. The New Testament Joseph too receives revelations in dreams and goes down to Egypt, the only New Testament figure to do so. If we combine the Genesis (Joseph) and Exodus (Moses) references, we get the following parallel: Old Testament Joseph/Pharaoh/Moses and New Testament Joseph/Herod/Jesus.

Slaughter of the innocents

Another motif common to the infancy narratives of Jesus and Moses is the *royal decree to kill all children* of a certain region in order to reach the hero of the account (cf. Ex 1:22; 2:1–10). This motif contains many parallel elements in the two narratives. In both there is an announcement which disturbs the peace of the king and his court: in Matthew, the inquiry of the wise men; in the legend about Moses, the dream of Pharaoh or the prediction of a scribe. In both stories the king decrees the death of all the children of a locality: in Matthew, the children born in Bethlehem during the last two years; in the Mosaic legend, all the male children who were born of the Israelites in Egypt. But in both cases the hero is saved by the intervention of God.

The *Targum of Jerusalem* on Ex 1:15 recounts a dream of Pharaoh in this way: 'Pharaoh while sleeping had a dream. Behold all the land of Egypt was placed on the pan of a balance scale, and a lamb, the son of a sheep, on the other pan; and the pan which carried the lamb was heavier. He commanded that all the wise men of Egypt be called and that this sign be recounted to them. Immediately Yanes and Yimbres, the chiefs of the wise men, took the word and said to Pharaoh, "A son is going to be born in the community of Israel who will destroy all of Egypt". For that reason, Pharaoh, the king of Egypt, gave the Jewish midwives the order of extermination.' Substantially the same legend is given in the *Chronicle of Moses* and by Josephus, though the latter ascribes Pharaoh's order to the prediction of a scribe.

We must note, however, that similar episodes concerning many infants are found in the histories of all peoples and in the legends of all literatures. The basis for all these legends is very simple: Everyone who has power is afraid on hearing the announcement of a possible rival, and attempts to get rid of the rival. This has occurred repeatedly among peoples of all times. The presence of these motifs in various stories as such neither refutes their historicity nor establishes literary dependence.

The star of the Magi

In Matthew the order for the massacre is occasioned by the report of the wise men, who say that they have seen a star in the East which has announced the birth of the king of the Jews. This star, however, has no literary connection with the theme of light shining in the room where a hero is born. It is probably not related, therefore, to the rays that according to the Moses legend illuminated the house where Moses was born, nor to the increase in the strength of the sun on the day of the birth of Isaac, nor to the luminous phenomena which usually accompany angelic apparitions and theophanies. However, a resemblance to Matthew's account of the star is found in the midrashic legend about the birth of Abraham.

One version runs like this. 'When our father Abraham was born, the astrologers said to their king Nimrod, "A son has been born to Terah; get hold of him and give him all he desires". Nimrod asked, "Why do you say this?" They answered, "We have seen that on the day he was born a star rose and devoured four stars in heaven; and this means that he will make himself master of two worlds".' Nimrod's interest in doing away with Abraham is clearly stated in a later legend. In this latter version Nimrod is told, 'Certainly a child has been born who is destined to conquer this world and the one to come. So give his parents all the money they ask of you for the child, and then kill it.' Terah, however, saved his son hiding him in a cave for three years. We should, however, note that the impossibility of assigning with certainty a date to those legends prior to the infancy narrative of Matthew reduces the probability that he was dependent on these legends.

Some scholars have thought that Matthew's account could be founded on the *Life of the Emperor Augustus* by Suetonius and on the story of the visit of Tiridates to Nero. On the other hand, Old Testament parallels have been found for the entire passage of the Magi. The motif of the star has been connected with the prophecy of Balaam: 'A star shall come forth out of Jacob, and a sceptre shall rise out of Israel' (Num 24:17). The messianic motif of light, which fills the entire Old

Testament literature, does play an important role in both Matthew's and Luke's infancy narrative, but it is always identified with the Messiah himself. The star of Jacob prophesied by Balaam is a personification. It is never understood as a celestial phenomenon, like the star in the story of the Magi. However, it must be said that these two symbolisms of a star are not always clearly distinguished in Israel's messianic expectation.

The flight into Egypt

Another motif found in Matthew is the *flight into Egypt*. The flight is completely logical, given the decree to slaughter the innocents. Even on the hypothesis that it is a simple literary motif, it would not be more than a minor episode within the more comprehensive motif of the persecution of the hero. We believe that this pericope draws on the Israel–Jesus typology. Jesus relives the Exodus experience of Israel. Some see here a direct influence of a *midrash* on Laban's persecution of Jacob (also called Israel), a *midrash* found in the liturgy of the Passover eve.

The *midrash* begins '. . . What did Laban the Aramean do to our father, Jacob? For Pharaoh decreed the destruction only of the males, while Laban sought to destroy my father, and he (my father) went into Egypt and sojourned there. . . . And he went down into Egypt, compelled by the word of the Lord. . . . And the Lord brought us forth from Egypt.' Matthew may also have in mind God's care for Moses, who twice escaped the persecution of Pharaoh. This is suggested by the final motif which is considered next.

The return from Egypt to Nazareth

The infancy narrative of Matthew closes with the passage of the *return to Nazareth*. The angel tells Joseph: 'Those who sought the child's life are dead' (Mt 2:20). Almost the same words are found in Exodus when God inspired Moses to return from Midian to Egypt: 'Go back to Egypt; for all the men who were seeking your life are dead' (Ex 4:19). The literary dependence extends to the detailed description of the trip: 'So Moses took his wife and his sons and set them on an ass, and went back to the land of Egypt' (Ex 4:20). The parallel in Matthew reads: 'And he rose, and took the child and his mother, and went to the land of Israel' (Mt 2:21). The evangelist has undoubtedly seen in this flight of Jesus into Egypt and his return to Nazareth a parallel with the flight of Moses into Midian and his return to free the people of Israel. The thought that Jesus is the true Son of God, typically symbolized in the people of Israel who were rescued from Egypt, also influenced Matthew.

We think that the primary typology in the infancy narrative is Jesus as Israel in its dual meaning of *Jacob-Israel* and *Israel as a nation*. The Jesus–Israel parallel is clearly expressed in Mt 2:15 with the help of Hos 11:1, 'When Israel was a child, I loved him, and out of Egypt I called my son'. This text deals with Israel's return from Egypt (the Exodus). The text of Hosea suggests that Jesus' return (Mt 2:19–21) should be seen as a replica of this exodus. The expression 'to the land of Israel' (Mt 2:20, 21) was no longer used in the time of Matthew and seems to point in the same direction: it recalls the promised land of the Israelites. Jesus relives the Exodus experience. As the head of the new Israel, the new people of God, Jesus reassumes the great experience of Israel, especially the Exodus, and thus brings history to its fulfilment. The presence of the double parallel should not surprise us. The same type of parallelism is found in the story of Jesus' temptations in the desert (Mt 4:1–11).

Literary form

More and more scholars believe that the literary genre of the infancy narrative is *haggadic midrash*, which was explained in Chapter One. This opinion is supported by (1) the likely influence of haggadic traditions about Jacob-Israel, Moses, and possibly Abraham (the star), (2) the presence of elements which are certainly legendary, and (3) the constant preoccupation with referring the Old Testament scriptures to Jesus, in whom they are fulfilled.

The description of *haggadic midrash* seems to fit Mt 1 – 2. There is only one difference, as has been noted when discussing the term *midrash* in Chapter One. We are not dealing with Old Testament events, but with New Testament events, the life and person of Jesus. In this connection, certain scholars have expressed some reservations about the use of the term *midrash* for the infancy narratives. But recent studies, as we have seen, point out that no Jewish scholar would restrict the term *midrash* so strictly. In Jewish tradition, *midrash* indicates many realities. The literary forms were not too clearly defined in Judaism. In order to indicate the special character of Mt 1 – 2, some suggest the term *Christian midrash*.

It would be quite false to consider the haggadic construction used by Matthew as synonymous with pure fancy. It is simply a free way of narrating history by adding picturesque details in order to highlight the theological teaching which is based on a few basically historical facts. It has been suggested that we call it *a moderate haggadic construction*, because the historicity of the central facts is certain. The names of the people involved, Jesus, Joseph, Mary, Herod, the Davidic ancestry of Jesus and, most probably, the birth in Bethlehem and residence at Nazareth appear to be historical facts. This leads us to some further considerations concerning the historicity of Mt 1 – 2.

Historicity

If Mt 1 – 2 is *midrash*, what can be said about an historical nucleus from which it has been developed? This question cannot be answered satisfactorily without extensive and detailed studies of the infancy narrative which, for the most part, are yet to be made.

An appraisal of the historicity of Mt 1 – 2 starts from two literary facts: Mt 1 – 2 has a complicated literary form, and this literary genus of Mt 1 – 2 is specifically *haggadic midrash*. *Haggadic midrash* means a free form of narration, in which picturesque details are not necessarily historical and the insertion of legendary elements is permissible. In fact such additions are rather expected, to accentuate the religious and theological meaning of the real facts. Hence we can immediately eliminate two extremes. On the one hand, historicity even in the smallest details would be practically excluded, and on the other hand, mere fiction or mere literary construction would be very unlikely.

It is very difficult, in the present stage of biblical scholarship, to determine the extent of the historical core in Mt 1 – 2, and we should not be astonished to find different opinions, even among Catholic scholars. Between the two extremes, mere fiction and historicity even in the details, several attitudes are possible. According to some, the amplification is secondary and Mt 1 – 2 has a high degree of historicity; others accept a higher degree of amplification and a rather limited historical core.

In a tentative evaluation of the historical nucleus of the infancy narrative, we can exclude certain elements as certainly legendary. These would be the extraordinary action of the star, the disturbance of all Jerusalem at the news of Jesus' birth and Herod's naive behaviour. In spite of his suspicions, he allows the Magi to go to Bethlehem without surveillance, so that they are able to find the child and leave the country without his knowing what they did. Herod's summoning the chief priests and the scribes is also highly improbable. Then, without the guiding star the visit of the Magi can be explained only on a series of unlikely hypotheses. For the rest, no single episode is in substance demonstrably unhistorical. However, the connections of Joseph's dreams, the flight and the massacre with the haggadic traditions suggest edifying amplification rather than fact.

The question of the historicity of Mt 1 – 2 cannot be settled by sentimental arguments, but only by a deeper study of the literary form of these texts. This was already the opinion of an eminent Catholic biblical scholar in the early part of this century:

> If it were necessary, one would see in these narratives a literary genre with its proper laws, to be interpreted according to these laws ... as an hors-d'oeuvre, a symbolic introduction to the activity of Jesus, Saviour of Israel and the Gentiles, rejected by Israel, accepted by the Gentiles.[8]

In this perspective it goes without saying that Matthew did not believe or wish to make others believe that everything which he states corresponds necessarily to actual events. It is almost certain that he included in his narrative certain elements, not because he considered them rigorously historical, but simply because he believed them peculiarly suited to throw into relief some aspect of the fundamentally historical event: the appearance of the Emmanuel, who was born of a virgin in Bethlehem in Judah, Light of the nations and the King of Israel, persecuted by evil, but finally victorious over both death and evil.

> The Infancy Narrative of Mt is a skilful composition of discrete traditions from various sources of varying (but overwhelmingly Jewish) provenance. The traditions reached Matthew in a high degree of literary elaboration (presupposing therefore a long and complex process of transmission), and they were further reinterpreted by him christologically through their integration into his messianically oriented Infancy Narrative. They are, then, religious not biographical traditions in their origin, inspiration, and intent, so that any historical information they provide is incidental, and does not appear to be of much worth.
>
> Genuine historical reminiscences may indeed underlie these traditions, but they are fugitive and not easily pinned down.[9]

Good on historicity

3   Who is the Messiah?

(Exegesis of Mt 1:1–25)

The genealogy of Jesus (Mt 1:1–17)

The evangelist introduces the whole narrative with a thematic headline: 'The book of the genealogy of Jesus Christ, the son of David, the son of Abraham' (Mt 1:1). Opinions are divided about what this sentence immediately refers to. Does Mt 1:1 refer to the genealogy immediately following? Does the sentence bear on the whole of Mt 1, on Mt 1 – 2, on the whole of Mt 1:1 – 4:16 or even on the whole of the gospel? All these opinions have their arguments.

The expression of Mt 1:1 reminds us of Gen 5:1, 'This is the book of the generations of Adam'. The parallelism is clear in the Greek text; both Mt 1:1 and Gen 5:1 use the expression 'The book of the genesis of . . .'. Matthew may have thought of Gen 5:1 and have intended to contrast the book of the origin of man with the origin of Christ.

Whatever the exact import of Mt 1:1 may be, in any case Matthew says that Jesus is 'the Christ' because he is the 'son of David'. And he is both of these because he is the 'son of Abraham'. This characterization of Jesus through the *names* Christ, son of David, and son of Abraham needs further explanation. This explanation is given in Mt 1 – 2, or even throughout the whole gospel.

The conception and birth of Jesus took place by a unique miracle. We read about it in the next section (Mt 1:18–25). Was it the effect of this miracle that Jesus stood apart from the natural bonds of family and nation? This is not a necessary conclusion. Through Joseph, who is legally his father, he enters a series of generations. By this Matthew testifies primarily that Jesus is true man. But further, the family in which he appears at a certain stage is a royal family, the house of David, the bearer of the messianic promises. Therefore, the first attribute given to Jesus the Christ is 'son of David'. The second attribute, 'son of Abraham' has a still wider scope. It is not only the royal line which culminates in Jesus. The list of ancestors is taken back as far as Abraham, the progenitor of the whole people, not only of one tribe. Above all, Abraham is the bearer of the ancient promises, 'by you all the families of the earth shall bless themselves' (Gen 12:3). This same idea finds expression in Mt 28:19, 'Go therefore and make disciples of all nations'. By opening his gospel with the genealogy of Jesus, Matthew sets out to describe the 'genesis of Christ', i.e., the insertion of the divine into human history.

The genealogy proper begins in Mt 1:2, 'Abraham was the father of Isaac'. Besides its faulty mathematics, Matthew's genealogy, if compared with Luke's, presents several discrepancies. Attempts to harmonize the two have been unsuccessful. It is rather through close study of the nature of biblical genealogy that the way is opened for a correct solution. The problem of the genealogies of Jesus can be solved if we realize that these passages belong to an Oriental literary form which is intended to convey a message, without being obliged to exactness in details.

The genealogy made use of the Old Testament insofar as it served the message of Matthew:

Mt 1:2   = I Chron 1:34; 2:1.
Mt 1:3   = I Chron 2:4, 5, 9.
Mt 1:4–6 = I Chron 2:10–15, 3:5.
Mt 1:7–11 = I Chron 3:10–15.
Mt 1:12   = I Chron 3:17–19; i.e. down to Zerubbabel.
Mt 1:13–16 has names otherwise not known to us in scripture, but they are names well enough known from Jewish sources of the Hellenistic period, including an increasing number of Aramaic documents.

The two climaxes

As we can see from Mt 1:1, there are two climaxes: Abraham and David. Mt 1:1 indeed summarizes the genealogy: 'The book of the genealogy of Jesus Christ, the son of David, the son of Abraham'. Mt 1:17 divides the history of the Old Testament into three periods, the first and the second of which begin with *Abraham* and *David* respectively. These three periods are: (1) from Abraham to the climax of the kingship in the person of David; (2) from David to the loss of the kingship during the Babylonian exile; (3) from the Babylonian exile to the messianic restoration of the kingship in Jesus, the Messiah. This shows that Matthew does not so much intend to give us a genealogical tree of Jesus, but rather a condensed history of Israel.

To these three periods corresponds Matthew's division of the genealogy into three equal parts each comprising fourteen generations. In order to obtain this triple balance, the writer had to omit the names of three kings and mention Jechoniah both as the last king of the pre-exilic series and as the first of the post-exilic series. By this means Matthew may have intended to underscore the royal Davidic lineage of Jesus, since fourteen is the numerical value of the Hebrew name *David*.[10]

Since fourteen is also the double of seven, some scholars have pointed out that we get six series of seven, a number that plays an important role in other passages of the gospel, so that Jesus would stand at the beginning of the seventh series. The meaning of this would be quite clear: since seven is the number of fullness, this place would mean that in him the fullness has its beginning.

Also the number seven and the title 'book of generation' allude pointedly to Genesis. Jesus' appearance in history is compared to a *new creation*, a new beginning of humanity and of the world. Whereas the generation of the fathers was imperfect, symbolized in the number six, Jesus inaugurated the perfect or seventh era.

At the same time this genealogy contains theological interpretations of the chosen people's vast history. Israel's history is seen as a prelude to Jesus the Messiah; he himself was the promise made to Abraham. In its present form Mt 1:2–17 forms a unity whose basic theme is that history has been a providential preparation for the coming of the Messiah. Jesus' genealogy, without pretending to be a summary of the entire gospel of Matthew, does nevertheless introduce its principal themes: the Messiah, the people of God, the fulfilment of the promises, the son of God, and eschatology.

The four women

Let us now concentrate for a while on one of the distinctive features of this genealogy. Contrary to the usual practice, the genealogy of Jesus in Matthew contains the names of four women: Tamar, Rahab, Ruth, and the wife of Uriah, Bathsheba. Why? An exegesis commonly accepted from patristic times onwards was that Matthew's mention of the names of these women was a sign that God came for the sake of sinners. However, neither Ruth nor Tamar is presented as a sinner, and so we should perhaps look for another quality which the four women have in common: not being Jews. Yet for at least one of them, Tamar, this hypothesis has no biblical foundation.

Another suggested reason for the inclusion of these women in Matthew's genealogy is the Hebrew traditions with which the evangelist was familiar. Taking Tamar as an example, Jewish legend has excused and even glorified her act of incest by attributing to her an ardent desire to be an ancestor of the Messiah. There is no doubt that the story of Tamar has been inserted into the book of Genesis (Gen 38:1–30) because of the posterity of Judah, ancestor of David and of the Messiah. The Jewish tradition unanimously places in relief the providential character of this narrative and strives to draw from it a profound meaning of the designs of God.

Especially useful for a study of this tradition is the *Palestinian Targum*. This represents probably the most ancient form of the tradition which has been preserved for us and constitutes a sort of join between the biblical text of Genesis and the later tradition. In this Targum, after Judah has recognized the three pledges as his own and declared Tamar innocent, a divine voice comes down from heaven and says: 'It is from me that this thing comes'. Following this manifestation of the divine will the tribunal acquits both of them. It also mentions the divine voice saying, 'Both of you are acquitted before the tribunal. This thing has come from God.' Note the similarity to Mt 1:20: 'For that which is conceived in her is of the Holy Spirit'.

In addition to the Targum, other rabbinical sources treat of the religious meaning of the narrative. The *Midrash Tanhuma* underlines in a special way the divine design and at the same time the mysterious meaning of the narrative. It juxtaposes the beginning of the biblical account, 'And Judah went down . . .' with the verse from Isa 55:8: 'For my thoughts are not your thoughts, neither are your ways my ways'. It indicates clearly the relation between the account and the coming of the Messiah: 'And Judah went down to prepare the way for the last redeemer, who is the Messiah king, because the Messiah king was to come from him.'

The *Midrash Rabbah* manifests the same preoccupation: '. . . and Judah busied himself with taking a woman. And the Holy One, blessed be He, was in course of creating the light of the Messiah king. . . .' The *midrash* is so taken with the thought that a providential design presides over this account that it does not hesitate to show the two personages, Judah and Tamar, as 'guided by the angels or the spirit of God'.

Clearly then, the Jewish tradition gave a messianic orientation to the story of Judah and Tamar. Such was the divine plan: it was necessary that Tamar should have children because it was from her that the Messiah was to come. This is already the meaning of the *Palestinian Targum*'s treatment of the birth of Tamar's son: 'But as he drew back his hand, his brother was born. Then the woman said, "Now have you made your way forth? It is your portion to be the stronger: It is you who will someday possess the kingship." And she named him Perez.' It is from this point of view, too, that the *midrash* explains the behaviour of Judah and Tamar; they acted with a view toward the Messiah king: 'When Judah said, "She is innocent", the Holy Spirit manifested himself and said, "Tamar is not a prostitute and Judah did not wish to give himself to fornication with her; the matter took place because of me in order that the King Messiah might rise up from Judah".' Tamar's desire to have a child of Judah's blood expressed her total submission to the Holy Spirit. She is considered in the *midrash* to be God's instrument assuring man's contribution to the providential preparations of the coming of the Messiah.

Thus, it seems that if the evangelist made room for Tamar in his genealogy, he did so because he knew the Jewish tradition which saw in Tamar not only an ancestor of Christ but also a woman who had ardently desired this grace, this participation in the messianic benediction. By clarifying the full religious meaning of the biblical account relative to Tamar, midrashic tradition can throw new light on the gospel text.

Research like this into contemporary Jewish literature at the time of the writing of the gospel has been extended to the other three women in the genealogy. The second woman mentioned, Rahab, the prostitute of Jericho (Josh 2:1–21), does not appear in the history of Israel as a prostitute, but as a woman who did everything possible to make God's plan succeed at a very important moment of its realization, namely the entrance into the Promised Land. It is, therefore, not surprising that the Jews of Jesus' time and also the early Christians (cf. Heb 11:31) represented her attitude as a model of faith. Moreover, Jewish tradition affirmed that she had acted under explicit invitation of the Holy Spirit: 'Some have said that the Holy Spirit rested on her before the Israelites arrived in the Promised Land'.

Ruth, the third woman in the genealogy, had a special place in Jewish thought and an official place among David's ancestors (Ruth 4:18–22). But what did she mean to Jesus' contemporaries? Again the *midrashim* help us. Several texts establish a connection between the incest mentioned in Gen 19:31–37 as the origin of Moab and the vocation of the Moabite Ruth as ancestor of the Messiah. *Midrash Bereshit Rabbah* on Gen 19:32 says: ' "Come, let us make our father drink wine". Rabbi Tanhuma said in the name of Samuel: the young girl said: "Let us receive offspring (seed) of our father". . . . Who is this? The Messiah king born of Ruth the Moabite.' Other passages also suggest that Ruth was enabled to be faithful to her vocation as ancestor of the Messiah through the intervention of the Holy Spirit.

Bathsheba found a place in Mt 1:6 through 1 Chron 3:5. She is, however, not present because of her sin with David. Rabbinic literature is unanimous in trying to excuse this fault. She is included in the genealogy of Matthew as having assured the royal lineage in the person of Solomon.

Summing up, we can say that thanks to Jewish literature, we can see what these four women have in common in Matthew's genealogy. They all share the irregularity through which their motherhood and the realization of the promise pass. They share a total submission to God's plan, however puzzling. Finally, they share the intervention of the Holy Spirit who revealed to them the originality of their mission and gave them the power to be faithful to their vocation. In a certain sense Mary's vocation is prepared and prefigured by the vocation of these four women.

Joseph's place in the genealogy

The formula 'A was the father of B, B was the father of C', which is a standard one in Old Testament genealogies or *toledoth* ('generations'), is disrupted in Mt 1:16, where instead of 'and Joseph the father of Jesus' we read 'Joseph the husband of Mary, of whom Jesus was born'. This shift in pattern clearly indicates that Matthew did not want to say that Joseph was the biological father of Jesus.

This leads to the final consideration in our study of this genealogy: Is there, as certain critics maintain, a conflict between the genealogy whose obvious purpose is to show that Jesus was a descendant of David, as the prophets had affirmed the Messiah to be, and the following section of Matthew's first chapter (Mt 1:18–25)? More directly, is there a conflict between the genealogy and Mt 1:16, where it is made clear that Joseph was not the Saviour's natural father?

That the evangelist knew very well what he was doing appears from the first verse: 'The book of the genealogy of Jesus Christ, the son of David, the son of Abraham' (Mt 1:1). The discerning reader is at once reminded of the way in which God promised offspring to these men. To David an heir would be born whose throne would be established forever (II Sam 7:13). Of this heir God said: 'I will be his father, and he shall be my son' (II Sam 7:14). In Jesus this is literally fulfilled. To Abraham an heir would be born beyond the natural powers of generation: 'Shall Sarah, who is ninety years old, bear a child?' (Gen 17:17). The birth of Jesus also transcended the laws of nature. It was God alone who made it possible for Sarah to have a child, and it was God who worked a similar, though greater, miracle in the case of the virgin Mary.

Matthew thus presents us with a paradox which had already been foreshadowed in the Old Testament: a son of Abraham who is really born through the intervention of God. The close relationship between the genealogy and the remainder of Mt 1 is, however, evident from Mt 1:20–21: 'Joseph, son of David, do not fear to take Mary your wife, for that which is conceived in her is of the Holy Spirit; she will bear a son, and you shall call his name Jesus'. The miraculous conception is described to Joseph but the angel instructs him to act as the father of the child and to acknowledge him as his own, for this is what is implied in the command 'You shall call his name Jesus'.

In the last two verses of the genealogy the Christ-Messiah is mentioned twice, and emphatically referred to: 'of whom Jesus was born, who is called Christ' (Mt 1:16) and 'from the deportation to Babylon to the Christ fourteen generations' (Mt 1:17). One of the aims of the genealogy is to prove the true messiahship of Jesus. It expresses what Matthew stresses throughout the whole gospel: Jesus is truly the promised Messiah. But by tracing the genealogy to Abraham in whom 'all the families of the earth shall be blessed' (Gen 12:3) Matthew shows right from the beginning that this Messiah is too great to be seen simply as a royal descendant of David.

The conception and birth of Jesus (Mt 1:18–25)

> . . . the role of Mt 1:18–25 in the over-all redactional pattern of
> the Infancy Narrative is not that of rebutting calumnies about the
> birth of Jesus, but that of explaining the riddle of the origin of
> Jesus presented by the aberrant ending of the Genealogy.[11]

Mt 1:18–25 is the least typical of the three dream narratives which
occur in the infancy narrative because of the combination of the dream
motif with a carefully structured 'command–execution' pattern which
is also found in Matthew's narrative of Jesus' entry into Jerusalem (Mt
21:1–7):[12]

	Mt 1:18–25		Mt 21:1–7
setting	18f. — When his mother Mary had been betrothed	1 —	And when they drew near to Jerusalem
command	20f. — Do not fear to take Mary your wife	2f. —	Go into the village opposite you
	— she will bear a son		— you will find an ass
	— and you shall call his name Jesus.		— untie them and bring them to me.
quotation	22f. — All this took place to fulfil what the Lord had spoken by the prophet.	4f. —	This took place to fulfil what was spoken by the prophet.
execution	24f. — When Joseph awoke from sleep, he did as the angel commanded him	6f. —	The disciples went out and did as Jesus had directed them
	— he took his wife		— they brought the ass
	— but knew her not		— and put their garments on them
	— and he called his name Jesus.		— and he sat thereon.

Since in Mt 21:1–7 the command–execution pattern has been imposed
on an earlier traditional account best preserved in Mk 11:1–7, the

same is most probably true of Mt 1:18–25. This does not mean that Mt 1:18–25 is wholly the work of the redactor or editor. Rather, a pre-existing dream narrative (Mt 1:20) which underlies the pericope has been combined with an annunciation story including a birth oracle (Mt 1:21), and fitted by the redactor into the command–execution pattern discussed above.

By his genealogy linking Abraham and David with the Messiah, the author has led his readers to expect an unusual birth narrative, and this he now proceeds to give. But the immediate circumstances of the event, the preparations for it, and the event itself are hardly presented at all. Matthew's attention is directed to completely different things. The core of Mt 1:18–25 is built from and, as much as possible, by means of the quotation: 'Behold, a virgin shall conceive and bear a son, and his name shall be called Emmanuel' (cf. Isa 7:14). We have, as it were, a recitative consisting in a progressive repetition of the theme: 'conceive' – 'bear a son' – 'call his name':

Isa 7:14	Matthew 1:20–21
shall conceive	that which is conceived
shall bear a son	will bear a son
shall call his name	you shall call his name

Beside this schema we have another one: the description of the message of the angel and its execution. The event occurs in three stages: the apparition (Mt 1:20), the message (Mt 1:20–21), the execution (Mt 1:24). We have here a schema which is repeated almost literally in Mt 2:13–15 and Mt 2:19–23:

	Mt 1:18–25	Mt 2:13–15	Mt 2:19–23
apparition	v. 20a	v. 13a	v. 19
message	vv. 20b–21	v. 13b	v. 20
execution	v. 24	v. 14	v. 21

In the message of Mt 1:20b–21 we have the classical Old Testament message style, used in the birth stories of great figures (see e.g., Gen 16 – 17; Judg 13:11–24; Isa 7:14–16; compare Lk 1:5–25; 1:26–38). The characteristics of this style are: the addressing of the person by name; the reassurance 'fear not'; allusion to the difficulty presented by the women's barrenness; the bearing of a son; the name-giving; and the establishment of the mission of this son by means of an explanation of the name. Thus Mt 1:18–25 is, as it were, a formal schema with a few individual elements, especially the names of the persons concerned: Jesus, Mary, Joseph.

Verse 18: Now the birth (*genesis*) of Jesus Christ took place in this way. When his mother Mary had been betrothed to Joseph, before they came together she was found to be with child of the Holy Spirit;

This verse refers back to the first verse of the genealogy (see the use of *genesis* and *Jesus Christ* in both verses) as well as to the unexpected departure from the usual pattern of the genealogy in Mt 1:16 which Matthew is now going to explain. Mt 1:18a is quite Matthean in style and so may be a redactional link composed to link the genealogy (Mt 1:1–17) and the annunciation to Joseph (Mt 1:18–25).

Mary's motherhood is the work of the Holy Spirit (compare the frequent references to the intervention of the Holy Spirit in the case of the women mentioned in Matthew's genealogy, above). Now how did Matthew understand the intervention of the Spirit at the incarnation? Matthew does not tell us much about it. The begetting by the Spirit is mentioned only casually, as a well-known fact. At most we might point to a certain stress on the word *genesis* ('birth', 'origin'). In Mt 1:18 the use of the word is all the more striking for being unexpected. It is rather *gennēsis* ('begetting') that should be used, and quite a number of manuscripts do not hesitate to make this 'correction'. The use of the word *genesis* must be explained as an influence from the Book of Genesis. Mt 1:1 begins the gospel with the very words of Gen 2:4: literally, 'the book of the genesis of heaven and earth' (*biblos geneseōs* . . .). Hence it might be inferred that Matthew attributed to the Spirit in the 'genesis' of Jesus the same role he had 'at the beginning' in the 'genesis of heaven and earth'. In that case Jesus' begetting by the Spirit in Mt 1:18 would correspond to the creative work of the Spirit in Gen 1:2. The birth of Jesus would constitute the advent of the new heaven and the new earth, of the new creation announced by the prophets (Isa 43:18f.; 65:17). This interpretation is quite likely. Yet it cannot be denied that the text touches only lightly on that theme. The point of the account seems to lie elsewhere, namely in the legal fatherhood of 'Joseph, the son of David'.

'When his mother Mary had been betrothed to Joseph. . . .' Jewish betrothals or espousals were very different from a modern engagement, which only prepares for a future contract. To the Jews, betrothal was the actual contract of marriage, as Philo, a Jewish philosopher who was a contemporary of Jesus, says: 'espousals have the force of marriage'. By virtue of espousals the parties gave each other rights; for instance, the husband could render null and void vows taken by his wife (Num 30:6–8 [7–9]); sexual intercourse with a third person was looked upon as adultery to be punished by stoning (Deut 22:23f.); if the husband died during betrothal the wife was considered a widow, etc. The period of betrothal lasted a year in the case of a virgin, or a month in the case of a widow. During this time, marital intercourse was considered illicit.

At the end of the period the marriage was solemnized by the husband taking his wife to his home. This was the occasion for the marriage feast.

> **Verse 19:** and her husband Joseph, being a just man and unwilling to put her to shame, resolved to send her away quietly.

There are three 'classic' theories about Joseph's state of mind at the time of the doubt:

(1) He suspected that Mary had committed adultery.
(2) While not suspecting her of adultery, he knew nothing of the miraculous conception, and so suspended all judgment.
(3) Mary's miraculous conception by the Holy Spirit had already been made known to him. Joseph feared to take Mary as his wife from awe at the greatness of the miracle worked in her.

(1) According to the first theory, after the *visitation* Joseph came to know that Mary was with child. Knowing that the child was not by him and knowing no more, he suspected Mary of adultery. As he was 'just' and did not want to make the matter public, he intended to give Mary a bill of divorce privately. There is a great difficulty in reconciling this theory with the fact that Joseph was 'just' (*dikaios*). Is Joseph called a 'just' man because he intended, according to a supposed law (most probably not rigorously enforced in New Testament times), to repudiate Mary and because he decided to do it secretly? Such interpretations seem to lack any literary, historical or theological basis. It is false to suppose that Joseph was caught in a dilemma as to whether or not Mary had committed adultery.

Joseph was failing in his duties if he suspected Mary and did not denounce her. Prominent Fathers of the Church held the theory of suspicion of adultery. But it must be noted that they only mention this view while treating some other subject. Most modern commentators do not accept the view that Joseph suspected Mary.

(2) According to the second view, Joseph comes to know that Mary is pregnant, remaining ignorant of the cause. He has such a high regard for her that he cannot suspect her. He suspends all judgment about her. In this mind he does not wish to make the matter public, but intends to divorce Mary secretly. This second theory fails to supply a sufficient reason for the fact that Joseph resolved to send Mary away. He is 'just', possessing all virtues, yet he 'fears' to take Mary his wife, even though he is certain that she is innocent!

(3) The third theory holds that when Joseph finds out the cause of Mary's pregnancy, he at first shrinks from taking the final step of

receiving into his household a person so intimate with God. This would be a natural reaction on Joseph's part, given that he had the Old Testament outlook of fear of God. The passage about Joseph wishing to repudiate Mary secretly presents a difficulty for all explanations. In this third theory, which postulates a thoroughly Old Testament attitude of fear in Joseph (cf. Lk 5:5; Mt 8:8), it can be understood why Joseph was minded to set Mary free. As will appear further, our explanation is close to this third theory.

According to some noted biblical scholars, Joseph knew the mystery that was taking place. Therefore, Mt 1:20–21 does not really inform him of the mystery. He knows it already. The meaning of these verses is that the angel assures Joseph that *despite* the virginal motherhood of Mary, he will still have to fulfil his fatherly mission toward the child. Joseph being himself a son of David (Mt 1:20), the child will also be a son of David to whom is promised his ancestor's throne. Thus Joseph proved his *justice* in the very fact that by marrying Mary he feared to trouble the mysterious vocation of his fiancée, manifested in her virginal motherhood. He is told by the angel that God wants him to take Mary into his home.

Other exegetes hold, against this view, that to say that Joseph's justice consisted in his unwillingness to be taken for the father of the child is unsatisfactory. Instead they suggest that 'just' be taken in the Hebrew sense, as equivalent to 'moderate' (Greek *metrios*), 'reasonable' (*epieikēs*), and 'benevolent' (*philanthrōpos*). The word 'just' would then draw attention to the balanced judgment of this holy man, and to the deliberation which preceded his decision.

Some believe that Gen 1 – 2 as well as Gen 5 – 6 served as models for the composition of Mt 1, and think that the term 'just' (*dikaios*) has been suggested by Gen 6:9, 'Noah was a righteous (*dikaios*) man'. In the New Testament Joseph is just, as Noah, who is called just 'by faith' in Heb 11:7, was just in the Old Testament. This supports the view which takes 'just' in the Hebrew sense.

The main objection to the third theory mentioned above is usually that the cause of Joseph's doubt (the fact that Mary is with child by the Holy Spirit) cannot be at the same time its solution. The angel, however, is not said to bring *information* to remove Joseph's doubt. He brings an *order* and supports it by the repetition of what Joseph already knows. It would then be the *order*, not any *information*, that resolves Joseph's doubt.

Verses 20–21: But as he considered this, behold, an angel of the Lord appeared to him in a dream, saying, 'Joseph, son of David, do not fear to take Mary your wife, for that which is conceived in her is of the Holy Spirit; (21) she will bear a son, and you shall call his name Jesus, for he will save his people from their sins.'

Except for a single instance in the passion narrative (Mt 27:19), references to dreams in the gospels are confined to the infancy narrative in Matthew. The question of the source for Joseph's dreams in Matthew naturally arises. A characteristic element in the history of the patriarchs is the frequency of dreams calling them to a vocation surpassing all human capabilities. The 'dream source' underlying this part of Matthew's infancy narrative is likewise concerned with the atmosphere of prodigy and wonder surrounding the person of Jesus, the course of whose earthly life was directed by God alone.

> Jesus is truly 'son of David' as the genealogy shows, a sonship the 'how' of which Mt 1:18–25 will spell out. The genealogy, however, being basically an OT witness, cannot do more than establish the divinely intended Davidic character of the Messiah. The fact that Jesus is 'God with us' comes not from the genealogy but from a divine revelation through 'an angel of the Lord.' . . . Joseph can acknowledge Jesus by naming him, and that makes him 'son of David'; the Holy Spirit has to act and God has to designate Jesus through revelation to make him 'Son of God.' . . . The 'How' of Davidic sonship is through the agency of Joseph. . . . For Matthew this is emphatically *God's will*, since the two steps in the legal paternity are dictated by the angel and carried out by Joseph exactly 'as the angel of the Lord had commanded him' (1:24). The first step is: 'Do not be afraid to take Mary your wife into your home.' . . . The second . . . : 'You will call his name Jesus.' By naming the child, Joseph acknowledges him as his own. . . . With much less detail Matthew narrates the 'How' of Jesus' other identity as 'God with us' or Son of God. This sonship is through the Holy Spirit.[13]

The main part of the angel's message seems to be the command, 'Do not fear to take your wife'. This is confirmed by the verses which follow the description of the dream, 'When Joseph woke from sleep, he did as the angel of the Lord commanded him; he took his wife'. Now if this command is the main purpose of the message, is it not possible that the angel adds the rest of the message, 'for what is conceived in her is of the Holy Spirit . . .', to win credence for the command?

We are often told that angels give signs in order to win credence (see Lk 1:20; 1:36; 2:12). Here the sign given is that the angel knows Joseph's thoughts and the secret message to Mary, repeating that message almost verbatim. There is a similar instance of an angel winning confidence in Mt 28:5, 'Do not be afraid; for I know that you seek Jesus . . .'.

'You shall call his name Jesus, for he will save his people from their sins.' Joseph has been emphatically designated a son of David because it is his task to hand on to Jesus the Davidic succession, which

takes place in the giving of the name. The Hebrew name *Jeshuah* or
Joshuah means 'Yahweh is salvation'; so, as Matthew points out, it is
applicable to Jesus who will save his people, Israel, from their sins.
There may be an echo here of Ps 130(129):8, 'And he will redeem
Israel from all his iniquities'.

> **Verses 22–23:** All this took place to fulfil what the Lord had
> spoken by the prophet: (23) 'Behold, a virgin shall conceive
> and bear a son, and his name shall be called Emmanuel'
> (which means, God with us).

The prospect of the longed-for king outlined by Isa 7, 9, and 11 was
never completely realized by Hezekiah, the child promised to Ahaz.
The prophet himself seems to have clearly recognized this. Despite the
shadows over Hezekiah's reign, he was, as a king, one of the most
perfect embodiments of the prophetic ideal which the Old Covenant
was to produce: 'There was none like him among all the kings of Judah
after him, nor among those who were before him. . . . the Lord was
with him' (II Kgs 18:5–7). In Hebrew, 'the Lord (Yahweh) was with
him' is perhaps an allusion to the title 'Immanuel'. Later, under
Manasseh, Amon, and the successors of Josiah, then during the
Babylonian exile and the Persian occupation, and finally under the
Hellenistic and Roman occupations, the memory of Isaiah's promise
was kept alive. Israel knew that Yahweh's will and power to save was
not limited to a distant past, and that his word never returns to him
without having achieved the aim for which he sent it (Isa 55:10–11).

The gospel of Matthew therefore uses this oracle of Isaiah. The
author clearly intends his readers to understand that Mary conceived
Jesus in a miraculous way. But the quotation of Isa 7:14 has a *much
wider scope* than that. The extraordinary circumstances surrounding
Jesus' conception and birth, the very name Jesus, so reminiscent of
Isaiah (*Jeshuah – Jesaiah*), the close parallelism between Mt 1:21 and
Isa 7:14, and the emphasis on the fact that 'he shall save his people
from their sins', all indicate that the reason for using the text of Isaiah
was to show that the promise of the royal Immanuel was at last fulfilled.
This was done in a manner transcending all previous expectations, in
the incarnation of Jesus, the son of David.

Since the evangelist was not claiming to be either an exegete or an
historian, he did not pretend to enter into the mind of the ancient
prophet whose oracles he adopted. On the contrary; he assumes a
prophetic role himself, and proclaims the good news that Jesus of
Nazareth has not merely lived up to, but has gone far beyond all that
Israel ever hoped or dreamed: 'Lo, I am with you (= I am Immanuel)
always, to the close of the age' (Mt 28:20). 'Emmanuel (God with us)'
and 'I am with you always' form an inclusion, that is, a passage framed
by two identical or very similar phrases, suggesting that in the coming

of Jesus the presence of God is experienced in a decisive and final (eschatological) way. God intervened several times in the genealogical record of the Messiah, as well as in the birth of people like Samuel and John the Baptist who were born of parents who in the normal course of events could no longer have had children. His intervention through the Spirit in the conception and birth of Jesus far supersedes all previous interventions, so much so that for the first and only time no human begetter can be named.

> **Verses 24–25:** When Joseph woke from sleep, he did as the angel of the Lord commanded him; he took his wife, (25) but knew her not until she had borne a son; and he called his name Jesus.

Non-Catholic scholars, like J. C. Fenton, author of the much-used commentary on Matthew in the Pelican Gospel Commentaries, agree that this verse need not necessarily imply that Joseph did know Mary *after* she had borne her son. But they refer to texts like Mt 12:46f., 'his mother and his brethren stood outside', and Mt 13:55f., 'And are not his brethren James and Joseph and Simon and Judas?' and say that these references to Jesus' 'brothers' and 'sisters' without further explanation suggest that Mary had other children.

Since the fourth or fifth century, however, it has usually been held that Mary had no children other than Jesus, and that the 'brothers' were either children of Joseph by a previous marriage, or cousins. Moreover, the implication of the English 'until' is not present in the Greek word *heōs*, and would be even less likely if a Semitic original lay behind the passage. Matthew's chief interest is in the affirmation that Joseph is not the natural father of Jesus, and that is what determines his language.

We should note here that in Matthew no annunciation is made to Mary. For Matthew, unlike Luke, the virginal conception is the basis rather than the subject of Mt 1:18–25. The birth itself is mentioned only briefly by Matthew, in two subordinate clauses, one in Mt 1:25, 'until she had borne a son', the other in Mt 2:1, 'Now when Jesus was born'.

As far as the problem of the virginal conception of Jesus is concerned, Raymond E. Brown would speak for the vast majority of Catholic exegetes when he says:

> . . . while Matthew and Luke apparently accepted the virginal conception as historical, we cannot be certain where they got their information on this point. The older thesis that all information in Luke's Infancy Narrative came straight from Mary's side of the family, while Matthew's information came from Joseph's side, is no longer tenable in modern exegesis – even though family origins

for some information cannot be *a priori* excluded. Consequently we must face the possibility that in good faith the evangelists have taken over an earlier belief in virginal conception that does not have an authentic historical basis. In short, the presence of the virginal conception in the Infancy Narratives of the two Gospels carries no absolute guarantee of historicity.[14]

And the same author terminates his study by saying:

My judgment, in conclusion, is that the totality of the *scientifically controllable* evidence leaves an unresolved problem. . . .[15]

4 The Destiny of the Messiah

(Exegesis of Mt 2:1–23)

The visit of the Magi (Mt 2:1–12)

Many exegetes call Mt 2 a *midrash* without specifying the biblical passages upon which the author is commenting. It has been suggested that Mt 2 is a *midrash* on Isa 41:2–3:

> Who stirred up one from the east
> whom victory meets at every step?
> He gives up nations before him,
> so that he tramples kings under foot. . . .

The possible interpretations and the different opinions which the rabbis propose for this prophetic passage and the succession of events in Mt 2 point in the direction of this passage from Isaiah. Possibly some early Christian preacher sought to explain the events surrounding the birth of Jesus in the light of Isa 41:2–3, interpreted according to the canons of traditional exegesis. Later the author of the Greek gospel of Matthew could have reworked this *midrash*, using his own literary forms and proof-texts.

The colourful and dramatic episode of the Magi contrasts sharply with the sober conciseness of the rest of Matthew's infancy narrative. It has been pointed out that Mic 5:2(1) is not a fulfilment or formula quotation, like the other quotations in the infancy narrative, but rather a *contextual quotation*. But it has been maintained that, although formally a contextual quotation, Mt 2:5–6 plays the part of a formula quotation and has been called 'a formula quotation by adoption'. There were in existence a number of other texts which could have been used as *fulfilment quotations*:

Ps 72(71):10:	May the kings of Tarshish and of the isles render him tribute, may the kings of Sheba and Seba bring gifts!
Ps 72(71):11:	May all kings fall down before him, all nations serve him!

Isa 49:7:	Kings shall see and arise; princes, and they shall prostrate themselves. ...
Isa 60:1–2:	Arise, shine; for your light has come, and the glory of the Lord has risen upon you. For behold, darkness shall cover the earth, and thick darkness the peoples; but the Lord will arise upon you, and his glory will be seen upon you.
Isa 60:3:	And nations shall come to your light, and kings to the brightness of your rising.
Isa 60:4:	Lift up your eyes round about, and see; they all gather together, they come to you; your sons shall come from far, and your daughters shall be carried in the arms.
Isa 60:6:	A multitude of camels shall cover you, the young camels of Midian and Ephah; all those from Sheba shall come. They shall bring gold and frankincense, and shall proclaim the praise of the Lord.
Num 24:17:	A star shall come forth out of Jacob, and a sceptre shall rise out of Israel.

The fact that, notwithstanding these many texts, Mt 2:1–12 does not make use of the *fulfilment quotation* technique has been taken by some to mean that Mt 2:1–12 has a different origin from the Joseph stories (Mt 1:18–25; 2:13–15; 2:19–23). It may have been inserted into these three stories which, as the evidence suggests, have a common origin.

It has been remarked as strange that Mt 2:1–12 does not refer to the visit of the Magi as a fulfilment of Ps 72(71):10–11, when in the rest of the infancy narrative Matthew seems to be looking for Old Testament passages he can use. The influence of Num 24:17 and Isa 60:1 is clear, but the only text selected for actual citation is Mic 5:2(1). This is not because it is vitally important for the story itself, for it only supplies the one detail that Bethlehem is to be the birthplace, but it seems that this detail had already assumed importance in contemporary apologetic concerning the origin of Jesus (from Bethlehem/from Nazareth: see below).

Possibly Matthew does not quote Ps 72(71):10–11 because the parallel he had in mind lay elsewhere, namely I Kgs 10:1–13, the story of the visit of the Queen of Sheba to Solomon. Jesus himself refers to this same parallel at a later date (Mt 12:42). As a symbol of Wisdom, Solomon had no rival in Israel. The Old Testament itself declared that his wisdom surpassed that of all men, even the Egyptians whose proficiency in this area was proverbial (I Kgs 4:29–31); and Hebrew legend also embroidered his wisdom with preternatural gifts. It was to see with her own eyes the wisdom of Solomon (I Kgs 10:7) that the Queen of Sheba journeyed to meet him. When her mission had been accomplished she exclaimed: 'Blessed be the Lord your God, who has delighted in you and set you on the throne of Israel'. And 'then she gave the king . . . gold, and a very great quantity of spices, and precious stones' (I Kgs 10:9–10).

How like Mt 2:1–12 this is! Perhaps too, the questioning by Herod in Mt 2:7–8 is not without relevance to this proposed parallel: in I Kgs 10:1 the Queen of Sheba comes to test Solomon 'with hard questions', all of which are answered beyond her expectation. In Matthew, Herod, through his ignorance of this central event in Israel's history and by reversing the role he should be playing, were he truly Solomon's successor, reveals himself as the antithesis of the Wisdom of God.

The Jewish *midrash* on the story of Solomon and the Queen of Sheba also incorporates the element of the star: 'As the Queen of Sheba approached the Holy City, reclining in her litter, she saw at a distance a wondrous rose growing at the edge of a lake. But when she came near she saw to her astonishment the rose suddenly transformed into a flashing star. The closer she came the more dazzling was its light.'

In all major respects, then, the parallel between the visit of the Magi to Jesus and that of the Queen of Sheba to Solomon is remarkably close. In both a star beckons; in both there are hard questions; in both the visitors acknowledge the divinely ordained royalty of the visited; and in both there is a lavish presentation of gifts. On one detail, however, the accounts differ. The Queen of Sheba was a woman *from the South* (see Mt 12:42); the Magi are men, a particular class of men *from the East* (Mt 2:1). Those who see the Magi episode as a simple *midrash* on the theme Jesus–Wisdom, as represented by Solomon, will have no difficulty in accounting for the change of this one detail. However, as will be seen below, a striking parallel for this detail is found in Num 22 – 24, the story of Balaam.

Some authors have suggested a connection between Matthew's story of the Magi and Cassius Dio's account of the visit to the emperor Nero by Tiridates, king of Armenia, who came from the East to Rome to pay homage in A.D. 66 (fifteen to twenty years before the writing of Matthew); he and his companions are elsewhere referred to as *magi*. However, because of the wealth of Jewish parallels, most authors do not consider this event a likely model for Matthew's account.

Another possibility is that the Magi story is a kind of commentary on Mt 8:11–12, 'I tell you, many will come from east (*apo anatolōn*; exactly the same expression as in Mt 2:1) and west and sit at table with Abraham, Isaac, and Jacob in the kingdom of heaven, while the sons of the kingdom (Herod and the chief priests and scribes?) will be thrown into the outer darkness'. The meaning of the story would then be: Jesus as the founder of the eschatological people of God is already revealed in the providential events of his childhood which forecast the future rejection by Israel and acceptance by the Gentile world.

The story of the Magi falls into two distinct parts, introduced by 'behold, wise men' (*idou magoi*; Mt 2:1b) and 'lo, the star' (*idou ho astēr*; Mt 2:9b). The first part, Mt 2:1–9a, is a dialogue centred chiastically (A-B-C-B-A) on the quotation of Mt 2:5–6, which is its structural centre as well as its logical climax.[16]

verses 1–2	A	Behold, *wise men* from the East *came* to Jerusalem, saying. . . .
verses 3–4	B	When *Herod* the king heard this, he was troubled, . . . and *assembling* all the chief priests and scribes of the people he *inquired of them* where the Christ. . . .
verses 5–6	C	They told him, 'In Bethlehem of Judea; for so *it is written* by the prophet . . .'.
verses 7–8	B	Then *Herod summoned* the wise men secretly and *ascertained from them* what time the star appeared. . . .
verse 9	A	When they (the *Magi*) had heard the king they *went* their way.

The second part, Mt 2:9b–12, is a linear narrative without any dialogue which moves at a high pace to its climax, the adoration of the child. It may have originated as a *midrash* on Isa 60.

These two parts were most probably originally independent traditions which have been redactionally joined together. The common motif of the star may have occasioned the combination of these two stories by Matthew or by the pre-Matthean tradition.

Verse 1: Now when Jesus was born in Bethlehem of Judea in the days of Herod the king, behold, wise men from the east came to Jerusalem.

The introduction to the second narrative of Matthew's infancy narrative shows a remarkable blend of continuity and discontinuity with the preceding narrative. For the first time we learn in Matthew that the birth of Jesus took place in *Bethlehem* in the land of *Judea*. Perhaps we would have expected this information already in Mt 1:18–25, if we were not aware of the role of the geographical names in the structure of Mt 1 – 2. Both *Bethlehem* and *Judea* fulfil the prophecy according to which the Messiah can be born only in the royal land of Judah, and in a city lying in this land. The two place names in Mt 2:1 already anticipate the Old Testament quotation which is given in full in Mt 2:6.

The word *Bethlehem* in Hebrew means 'house of bread' or 'city of food'. It is the name given to two cities in Palestine, one in the territory of Zebulun (Josh 19:15; Judg 12:8, 12), the other in the territory of Judah (Mic 5:2[1]). Both still exist today, the first in Israel, the second in Jordan (but since 1967 under Israeli occupation). The modern Arabic name for both is *Beit-lam*, 'house of meat'. Bethlehem in Judah, sometimes also called *of Judea* (Mt 2:1, 5), plays an important role throughout the Old Testament, where it is mentioned thirty-six times in twelve different books. In the Bible this Bethlehem is sometimes also called *Ephrata* (Gen 35:19; Ruth 4:11; Mic 5:2[1]); the word is also Hebrew and means 'fruitfulness' or 'fertility'. Bethlehem and Ephrata are therefore in a certain sense synonymous. Their identification, or even substitution for each other, whether by choice or by accident, is readily understandable.

Bethlehem, though in itself a comparatively small and unimportant rural village, plays an important role through the entire course of Old Testament history. The significance of its role is highlighted when the various episodes recounted about the city are listed together. Bethlehem is then seen to play a special part in each successive stage of the history of the chosen people, from the time of Abraham's calling to the coming of the longed-for Messiah.

In the *period of the patriarchs* there is the story of Rachel's death and burial (see Gen 35:19 and Mt 2:18). According to another tradition, Rachel was buried in the territory of Benjamin, not Judah (see I Sam 10:2). It is possible that a later editor of Genesis may have connected the burial place with Bethlehem in order to give more glory to the birthplace of David. In that case we have an even stronger indication that Bethlehem was of special significance to the people of the Old Testament. As we shall see, the author of the gospel of Matthew follows the tradition contained in Genesis.

The role of Bethlehem during the period of the *conquest under Joshua* and of the *Judges* is not spectacular. Yet it does have a special quality of its own (I Chron 2). It appears to have been a Levitical city (Judg 17, 19; Num 35:1–8; Josh 21).

The *establishment of the monarchy* was a major event with far-reaching results for Israel. Of all the Israelite kings David was unquestionably the most favoured and beloved. The books of Ruth (1:1;4:11), I Samuel (16:4, 13, 18), and I Chronicles (11:16f.) are profuse in their efforts to connect Bethlehem with David, even to the extent of preserving parallel stories which differ considerably in detail (e.g., I Sam 16 – 17).

From the *period of the prophets* we have the reference to Bethlehem best known to most Christians today, as it was to the Jews in the time of Jesus: Mic 5:2(1). To this city will be given the unique honour of being the birthplace of the Saviour of mankind. No other city of Israel or in any other land will ever be as *fruitful* (*ephrath*) as Bethlehem, the *house of bread*.

After this, the name of Bethlehem does not occur again in the biblical narratives until the time of the *Babylonian captivity* (Jer 41:17). A group of people from Bethlehem are mentioned specifically among the exiles returning under Zerubbabel during the last quarter of the sixth century B.C. (Ezra 2:21; Neh 7:26).

It is important to note that all references to Bethlehem in the Old Testament are somehow recalled or incorporated by Matthew. He cites the prophecy of Micah designating Bethlehem as the birthplace of the new ruler (Mt 2:6 = Mic 5:2[1]). The royal character of the child is underlined by the quest of the Magi for the newly born 'king of the Jews' (Mt 2:3). As he recorded this visit, Matthew may well have had in mind a *royal* psalm: 'May the kings of Tarshish and of the isles render him tribute, may the kings of Sheba and Seba bring gifts! May all kings fall down before him, all nations serve him!' (Ps 72[71]: 10–11). The fulfilment of these prophecies gives a royal character to the city of Bethlehem; both the child and his visitors have kingly status.

The seer Balaam, whose story is found in Num 22 – 24, may have been the prototype of the 'wise men' or magi *from the East* (*apo anatolōn*). Balaam was by profession an interpreter of dreams and, therefore, a 'magus' (Philo), coming 'from the East' (*ap' anatolōn*, Num 23:7 in the Septuagint Greek), more particularly from Mesopotamia, the same land from which the Magi in Matthew would probably have come. While biblical tradition in general adopted a hostile view of Balaam, in Num 22 – 24 he is looked upon in a positive way. Balaam came from the East accompanied by two servants (Num 22:22) who in the *Palestinian Targum* become fellow-magi, thus forming a party of three. The hostile king Balak intended to use the foreign magus Balaam (and his two companions) to destroy his enemy, but the magus honoured Balak's enemy instead. This is very close to the story of Herod and the Magi. In fact both stories also end with the departure of the main characters: 'Balaam rose, and went back to his place' (Num 24:25), while the Magi 'departed to their own country' (Mt 2:12).

Verse 2: 'Where is he who has been born king of the Jews? For we have seen his star in the East, and have come to worship him.'

It is possible that we should render this verse: 'Where is the born (new-born) king of the Jews?' In the latter reading the astrologers are mainly concerned with the *where* of Jesus' birth, and emphasis is not so much on the *who*, the great one, newly born.

'We have seen his star'. There are many instances in ancient belief of special heavenly manifestations heralding the birth of great rulers. Efforts to explain the star as a natural phenomenon are quite unconvincing.

It is probable that the star is a legendary development. But from what source was this feature drawn? Some have thought of Num 24:17, 'A star shall come forth out of Jacob'. But in this text the star is a personification of the Davidic monarchy, whereas in Mt 2:2 it is an astronomical phenomenon. In principle, a midrashic use of the text could explain the transformation of the original reference to a person into an actual star. It is true that later Jewish writings often interpret the star in Num 24:17 as a symbol of a person, not a sign of his coming, but it allows of a literal fulfilment (a star) as well as a symbolical one (the Messiah). It should not be overlooked that nowhere else do we find a similar combination of a magus (magi) and a star. Moreover, in view of the many references to the star of Num 24:17 in Jewish tradition, it is difficult to see how the star of the Magi could fail to allude to it. Nevertheless, the difficulties mentioned make some scholars look elsewhere for a solution. Some have noted the striking resemblance to the midrashic stories of a similar phenomenon at the birth of Abraham (see Chapter Two above). This parallel may have been taken into account by Matthew, who writes about Jesus, 'the son of Abraham' (Mt 1:1). Others have referred to the star mentioned in the story of the Queen of Sheba's visit to Solomon.

We have seen his star 'in the East'. Only with difficulty can the Greek expression *en tēi anatolēi* mean 'in the East'. The correct translation is most probably 'at its rising'. What we appear to have here is a technical expression for the beginning of the phenomenon observed by the Magi. This refers to the belief of astrologers that every child is born under a certain astral combination, or, that everybody has *his star*. It is the star rising at the moment of birth that determines the horoscope. Now, among the texts found at Qumran there is a horoscope of the expected Messiah. In Jewish circles which believed in astrology there was apparently speculation about the star under which the Messiah would be born. Once they noticed the astronomical combination believed to be that under which the expected Messiah would be born, they would start looking for his birthplace, *where* he was born.

Verses 3–4: When Herod the king heard this, he was troubled, and all Jerusalem with him; (4) and assembling all the chief priests and scribes of the people, he inquired of them where the Christ was to be born.

Herod and 'all Jerusalem' do not rejoice at the news, but they are 'troubled'. The word is used again in Mt 14:26 to describe the terror of the disciples. In both cases it is a fear which comes from unbelief. Herod assembles the Sanhedrin, the supreme council of the Jews. Historically speaking, this is very improbable. Rather there may be a reference here to Ps 2:2, 'The kings of the earth set themselves, and the rulers take counsel together, against the Lord and his anointed . . .'.

Herod and the council are contrasted with the Magi. By their knowledge of nature, these visitors from the East discover the author of nature at Bethlehem, while Herod and the whole of Jerusalem search the scriptures and are unable to find the child. Herod's dark

anxiety, which is shared by those around him, when the Magi speak of
the newly born king, is like the reaction of the Jewish leaders during
Jesus' messianic entry into Jerusalem. Contrasting sharply with
Herod's anxiety is the joy of the Magi (Mt 2:10).

The Magi may be understood, not only as mysterious men from
the East who visited Jesus in Bethlehem, but as *representatives* of the
Gentile Christians of the first century A.D. And Herod may be understood, not only as a suspicious and hostile king who tried to kill the
infant Messiah, but also as the *representative* of Jewish hostility to the
new Church in those years of its beginnings in Palestine. It seems likely
that the author of Mt 2 actually had this representative quality in mind
when he wrote as he did about the Magi and Herod.

> **Verses 5–6:** They told him. 'In Bethlehem of Judea; for so it is
> written by the prophet: (6) "And you, O Bethlehem, in the
> land of Judah, are by no means least among the rulers of
> Judah; for from you shall come a ruler who will govern my
> people Israel." '

The opening words of the prophecy are quoted from Mic 5:1 (Hebrew
text, corresponding to Mic 5:2 in the Greek text), but the rest of the
text is neither a literal quotation of the Greek version nor an exact
rendering of the Hebrew text. Properly speaking, it is far from being a
quotation. It appears to be a Matthean combination of a rather original
kind.

Of the twenty-four Greek words in the *quotation*, only eight
render original Hebrew terms of the prophet Micah (5:1, 3[Greek 5:2,
4]), and it has only ten words in common with the Septuagint Greek
Bible. The most striking addition to the Hebrew as well as to the Greek
text is the strong negation 'by no means' (*oudamōs*) and the participle
'for' (*gar*), the textual source of which cannot be found. After 'from
you shall come' (*exeleusetai*), Matthew uses an element which cannot
be found in Micah and comes almost certainly from II Sam 5:2, 'you
shall be shepherd (*poimaneis*) of my people Israel, and you shall be
prince (*hēgoumenon*) over Israel'.

Combining Old Testament passages was a regular feature of
rabbinic study of the scriptures. We should, however, not overlook the
fact that Mic 5:4[3] reads 'He shall feed (Greek: *poimanei*) his flock'.
This verbal form *poimanei* may have been the *key-word* which
attracted II Sam 5:2 and its context, namely the account of David's
anointing at Hebron as chief (*hēgoumenos*) of Israel. The association
chief–shepherd is interesting and we should remember that in the Old
as well as in the New Testament the shepherd is the image of the king
governing his people.

> **Verses 7–9a:** Then Herod summoned the wise men secretly
> and ascertained from them what time the star appeared; (8)

and he sent them to Bethlehem, saying, 'Go and search diligently for the child, and when you have found him bring me word, that I too may come and worship him.' (9) When they had heard the king they went their way;

Herod inquired about the date of the appearance of the star. Then he sent the Magi to Bethlehem, and told them to return to him with information which would allow him also to go and worship the king. The verb 'ascertained' translates a Greek technical term used in astronomical observations. Matthew is preparing for Herod's order in Mt 2:16 to massacre all the boys 'of two years of age and under'.

Verses 9b–10: and lo, the star which they had seen in the East went before them, till it came to rest over the place where the child was. (10) When they saw the star, they rejoiced exceedingly with great joy;

The star leading the Magi to the place where the child was recalls the guidance of the Israelites in the wilderness by the pillar of cloud. This cloud went before the people showing them the way, and stood before the door of the tent sanctuary while the people worshipped. The star is the symbol of the divine guidance of the Magi. Attempts of modern science to identify it with known astronomical phenomena, such as the conjunction of the planets Jupiter and Saturn in 7 B.C., have proved inconclusive.

Verse 11: and going into the house they saw the child with Mary his mother, and they fell down and worshipped him. Then, opening their treasures, they offered him gifts, gold and frankincense and myrrh.

The 'house' referred to is the home of Joseph and Mary as inhabitants of Bethlehem. Matthew's view is very different from that found in Lk 2:1–7. The verb 'worship' (*proskunein*), found thirteen times in Matthew, is a favourite term and a characteristic feature of this gospel. Detailed symbolic meanings have been found in the gifts which the Magi offered from their treasure-boxes. They may, however, just be gifts suitable for presentation to a king: 'Long may he live, may gold of Sheba be given to him' (Ps 72[71]:15); 'They shall bring gold and frankincense, and shall proclaim the praise of the Lord' (Isa 60:6); 'Your robes are all fragrant with myrrh and aloes and cassia' (Ps 45[44]:8). The three gifts of the Magi are also mentioned in the Book of Revelation (18:11–13): 'And the merchants of the earth weep and mourn for her, since no one buys their cargo any more, cargo of *gold*, silver, jewels and pearls, fine linen, purple, silk and scarlet, all kinds of scented wood, all articles of ivory, all articles of costly wood, bronze, iron and marble, cinnamon, spice, incense, *myrrh*, *frankincense*, wine, oil . . .'.

In the centre of Mt 2 stands 'the child with (Mary) his mother' (Mt 2:11). This phrase is repeated four times (Mt 2:13, 14, 20, 21), and becomes, as it were, the leitmotif.

> **Verse 12:** And being warned in a dream not to return to Herod, they departed to their own country by another way.

Similar warnings using the passive of the verb *chrēmatizō*, 'instruct', are mentioned in Mt 2:22; Lk 2:26; Acts 10:22 and Heb 8:5. The fact that no angel is mentioned in Mt 2:12 and 22 is taken as an indication that these verses did not belong to the pre-Matthean narrative of angelic dream appearances. Departure by another route also occurs in Cassius Dio's account of the visit to Nero by Tiridates, mentioned earlier.

> The story is thus a proleptic working out of the tragic paradox which will be the theme of Matthew's Gospel, that Jesus born as the Son of David in David's city, fulfilling every OT prophecy, is yet rejected by his people . . . only to be honoured . . . by the gentiles.[17]

> . . . the christological moment (i.e., the moment of the revelation of who Jesus is – the Messiah – the Son of God in power through the Holy Spirit), which was once attached to the resurrection and then to baptism, has in the infancy narratives been moved to the conception: it is the virginal conception that serves now as the begetting of God's Son. . . . If the sequence of christological revelation, proclamation, and twofold reaction was verified in relation to the resurrection and the baptism, it is not surprising that it holds true in the infancy narrative as well. . . . Thus understood, ch. 2 is the necessary completion of ch. 1 in the sequence of revelation, proclamation, and twofold reaction, a sequence that gives the infancy narrative its status as a gospel in miniature.[18]

The flight into Egypt (Mt 2:13–15)

Mt 2:13–15 is a Matthean revision of a substantially pre-Matthean narrative whose structure and phraseology are strongly reminiscent of the Old Testament, more particularly the dream messages in Genesis. In fact, the dream of Jacob at Beersheba (Gen 46:2–4) may have served as the overall model for Mt 2:13–15 and the other dream narratives in Matthew. Besides, Rebekah's plea in Gen 27:43–45 may have served as a model for the angel's message in Mt 2:13, while I Kgs

11:40, which describes the flight of Jeroboam from Solomon, did the same for the execution of the message in Mt 2:14. The use of Hos 11:1 in Mt 2:15 was probably inspired by its allusion to the 'infancy' of Israel at the time of the Exodus, which suggested an application to the infancy of Jesus. It is undoubtedly intended as a justification for the Egyptian sojourn of the child Jesus.

> **Verse 13:** Now when they had departed, behold, an angel of the Lord appeared to Joseph in a dream and said, 'Rise, take the child and his mother, and flee to Egypt, and remain there till I tell you; for Herod is about to search for the child, to destroy him.'

The clause 'now when they had departed' constitutes the redactional link with the Magi story. The verb 'depart' (*anachōrein*) is characteristic of Matthew's style and thought. It is found ten times in Matthew, against once in Mark (3:7), once in John (6:15), and twice in Acts (23:19; 26:31). In several passages it refers to a situation in which Jesus departs or moves on from one place to another because of danger or unbelief encountered in the first place (see Mt 2:22; 4:12; 12:15; 14:13; 15:21). The reason for the angel's command is that Herod has made up his mind to search for the child. The verb 'to destroy' appears also in the passion narrative: 'Now the chief priests and the elders persuaded the people to ask for Barabbas and destroy Jesus' (Mt 27:20).

> **Verses 14–15a:** And he rose and took the child and his mother by night, and departed to Egypt, (15) and remained there until the death of Herod.

Herod's power would not extend to Egypt, which was a classic land of refuge for those fleeing from tyranny in Palestine (see I Kgs 11:40; Jer 26:21). The best evidence favours March/April 4 B.C. as the time of Herod's death. The words of the angel (Mt 2:13) and the execution of the command (Mt 2:14–15a) seem to be formulated with a view to the quotation from the Old Testament.

> **Verse 15b:** This was to fulfil what the Lord had spoken by the prophet, 'Out of Egypt have I called my son.'

The quotation is from Hos 11:1. It referred originally to God's calling Israel, his son, from Egypt at the time of the Exodus. Matthew, in contrast with the Septuagint, renders an exact translation of the Hebrew text. The Septuagint has: 'Out of Egypt I have called them sons'. The Matthean form of the prophecy is necessary for its function as a messianic proof-text in the context of the gospel.

The quotation is meant, it would seem, to suggest to the reader that the Messiah, himself the personification of the true Israel, repeated in his own life story the experience of the old Israel; and also that he was a second and greater Moses. His supreme work of salvation had as its prototype the mighty acts of salvation worked by God through Moses on behalf of his chosen people. And as Moses was called to go to Egypt and rescue Israel, God's son, his first-born (see Ex 4:22) from physical bondage, so Jesus was called out of Egypt to save mankind from the bondage of sin.

The massacre of the innocents (Mt 2:16–18)

The narrative is very compact. The core of the story, the description of the massacre, 'Then Herod . . . was in a furious rage, and he sent and killed all the male children in Bethlehem' (Mt 2:16b), is expanded by a circumstantial account of the site of the massacre and the age-group of its victims, 'and in all that region who were two years old and under' (Mt 2:16c). This is preceded and followed by two explicit allusions to the Magi story, 'when he saw that he had been tricked by the wise men' (Mt 2:16a) and 'according to the time which he had ascertained from the wise men' (Mt 2:16d), which integrate the narrative into the infancy narrative of Matthew. The formula quotation (Mt 2:17–18) is attached to the narrative (Mt 2:16) by links which are largely external. The first is a tradition about the location of Rachel's grave in Bethlehem (Gen 35:19; 48:7). Secondly, an allusion to Israel as God's beloved child in the context of Jer 31:15 (see Jer 31:20 with its reference to 'Ephraim my dear son', i.e. Israel). This allusion, like that of Hos 11:1, would make the text very applicable to the infancy of Jesus.

> **Verse 16:** Then Herod, when he saw that he had been tricked by the wise men, was in a furious rage, and he sent and killed all the male children in Bethlehem and in all that region who were two years old or under, according to the time which he had ascertained from the wise men.

The angel's warning (verse 13) is now fulfilled. In Exodus the Pharaoh is said to have issued a decree ordering the slaughter of all Israelite boys at birth. According to the *midrashim* the decree was inspired by the advice of magi (astrologers) and was intended to eliminate Moses. This is not, however, found in the biblical text, which presents the slaughter of the boys as intended to break the growth and the force of Israel. The midrashic presentation is paralleled in the story of Herod and the Magi (astrologers) and the decree to murder the male children in order to eliminate Jesus. It is interesting to note that an apocalyptic writing, *The*

Ascension of Moses, speaks of Herod and draws a parallel between the murders committed by Herod in order to eliminate rivals, and Pharaoh's murders to eliminate his rival, Moses. These traditions about Moses were very much alive in Matthew's time, and application to contemporary or recent events was by no means excluded.

The picture of the massacre is quite impressive, but it has been calculated that if Bethlehem had a thousand inhabitants (which is a high estimate), it would have had about thirty births per year, fifteen of them boys, half of whom would have died within a few days. Over a period of two years, then, we are left with about fifteen candidates for the massacre! All this, and especially the Old Testament quotation, gives the whole story the appearance of a catechetical instruction or homily rather than a documentary composition.

Verses 17–18: Then was fulfilled what was spoken by the prophet Jeremiah: (18) 'A voice was heard in Ramah, wailing and loud lamentation, Rachel weeping for her children; she refused to be consoled, because they were no more.'

The original context of the quotation from the prophecy of Jeremiah (31:15) speaks of Rachel, the mother of Joseph and Benjamin, weeping over her 'children' who are the exiles taken into captivity. Jer 31:15 is clearly addressed to Ephraim and so commemorates the catastrophe of 722–721 B.C., the captivity and deportation of the tribes of the Northern Kingdom by the Assyrians. But some scholars think that there is a possibility that Jeremiah is referring especially to the Benjaminites whose fate was entwined with the Southern Kingdom of Judah, overrun by the Babylonians in 587 B.C. It has been noted that Jer 40:1 tells us that after the fall of Jerusalem in 587 B.C. the captives from Jerusalem and Judah were taken to Ramah.

As we said before, there was a connection with Bethlehem, in that Rachel's grave was believed to have been there (Gen 35:19). Ramah was about six miles north of Jerusalem, on the road which the exiles would take. Herod's massacre of the children is related to Jeremiah's interpretation of the exile. It is a tragic passage which unexpectedly sounds a note of joy and introduces the famous description of the New Covenant (Jer 31:15–34).

The quotation should indeed be read in the context in which it is originally found. It is often necessary to do this in studying the quotations from the Old Testament found in the New Testament, for the biblical authors often understood the particular verses or sentences quoted as pointers to the whole context rather than as testimonies in themselves. Matthew transfers Jeremiah's scene to Bethlehem in order to recall this Old Testament promise of the New Covenant soon to be inaugurated in and by Jesus.

The return from Egypt and settlement at Nazareth (Mt 2:19–23)

Mt 2:19–23 is made up of two distinct parts. The first part, Mt 2:19–21, is constructed like the dream narrative of Mt 2:13–15 and is characteristically sparing in details of time and place. It is pre-redactional in origin and seems to have been patterned on the account of the return of Moses from his exile in Midian (Ex 4:19–20). The second part, Mt 2:22–23, is a novelistic travel account. It has been attached, as the immediate context of the formula quotation (Mt 2:23b), to the originally independent dream narrative (Mt 2:19–21) which narrated, as the counterpart of Joseph's flight into Egypt, the return of Joseph from exile. Mt 2:22–23 is apparently a redactional composition which contains the single traditional datum that Joseph settled in Nazareth because Archelaus was ruling in Judea.

> **Verses 19–21:** But when Herod died, behold, an angel of the Lord appeared in a dream to Joseph in Egypt, saying, (20) 'Rise, take the child and his mother, and go to the land of Israel, for those who sought the child's life are dead.' (21) And he rose and took the child and his mother, and went to the land of Israel.

Herod died in 4 B.C. The system of dating A.D. which was worked out by a sixth-century Christian monk called Dionysius the Small wrongly accepted the year 753 after the founding of Rome as the date of the incarnation. Jesus is most likely to have been born in the year 6 B.C.

When the Pharaoh died, Moses was told to return to Egypt. So now that Herod is dead, Joseph is told to bring Jesus back to Israel. 'For those who sought the child's life are dead' is a free quotation from Ex 4:19, where God says to Moses: 'Go back to Egypt, for all the men who were seeking your life are dead'. The plural 'those who sought' does not fit well into the context referring to the death of Herod. It is explicable only as due to the quotation. The phrase 'to the land of Israel' which occurs only here in the whole New Testament, also points to the Exodus and the time of Moses (see Ez 20:36–38). All this makes the verbal coincidences with the Septuagint version of Ex 4:19 a striking allusion. It is another indication for the secondary parallelism between Jesus and Moses. The primary parallelism remains that between Jesus and Israel.

> **Verse 22:** But when he heard that Archelaus reigned over Judea in place of his father Herod, he was afraid to go there, and being warned in a dream he withdrew to the district of Galilee.

Apparently, the information which Joseph received concerning Archelaus did not come from revelation, unlike his other information. This may very well indicate that verses 22–23 were added by Matthew to a substantially pre-Matthean account which originally ended with verse 21. The pattern, the grammar, and the vocabulary of Mt 2:22–23 are clearly the same as those of Mt 4:12–14. Since the latter is indisputably Matthean, the former is almost certainly also Matthean.

Archelaus was the son of Herod the Great who reigned over Judea from 4 B.C. to A.D. 6; Herod Antipas, another of Herod's sons, who is mentioned later in the gospel (Mt 14:1–12), reigned in Galilee from 4 B.C. to A.D. 39. It is not clear why Joseph is to go to the district of Herod Antipas instead of that of Archelaus. The only explanation seems to be the prophecy given in the next verse. We could, however, also refer to the prophecy of 'Galilee of the Gentiles' in Mt 4:12–16, and the fact that we are told that Jesus departed and withdrew (*anechōrēsen*, exactly the same term as here in Mt 2:22) into Galilee. There too Matthew's use of 'departed' or 'withdrew' (Mt 4:12) can hardly be meant as an indication that Jesus was leaving the jurisdiction of Herod Antipas, where John had been arrested, for Herod held sway over Galilee too.

Verse 23: And he went and dwelt in a city called Nazareth, that what was spoken by the prophets might be fulfilled, 'He shall be called a Nazarene.'

The quotation which the evangelist states was fulfilled in the residence of Jesus in Nazareth, has long been an enigma, for no such words are found anywhere in the Old Testament. The fact that the evangelist introduces the statement as having been 'spoken by the prophets' may be an indication that he did not intend to make an exact verbal quotation, but to point out in general terms that it was entirely in accordance with what the prophets had foretold, that Jesus should come to be known as Jesus of Nazareth.

To solve the problems concerning the biblical allusion 'He shall be called a Nazarene', one should distinguish three distinct, though related, questions. Firstly, what is the real historical origin of the term *Nazōraios*? Secondly, how did Matthew understand the term in his gospel? Thirdly, what biblical passage(s) does he refer to when he presents the title as fulfilled prophecy?

The origin of *Nazōraios*, an appellation of Jesus widespread in the gospels and Acts, has been explained by some as an adjective derived from *Nazara*, a Greek form of 'Nazareth' attested in the gospels, although this explanation fits its equivalent *Nazarēnos* better. Others have sought an explanation in postulating Jesus' membership of the elusive pre-Christian sect of Nazirites or Nazirates, or in a 'nazirite' Christology which saw Jesus prefigured in the great 'nazirs' dedicated to God in the Old Testament (e.g. Samson: see Judg 13:5; 16:17). It seems best to understand *Nazōraios* as the Greek rendering of the Aramaic *nāserāyā*, derived from the place name *nāzerat* and meaning 'from Nazareth'.

Matthew definitely understood *Nazōraios* as an adjective referring to Nazareth, that is, equivalent to his 'from Nazareth' (Mt 21:11; compare Jn 1:45; Acts 10:38).

The final statement of Matthew's infancy narrative affirms two things. Firstly, that the Old Testament predicts that Jesus is to be called *Nazōraios*. Secondly, that this prediction is fulfilled by the fact that Nazareth is the home town of Jesus. But which text(s) is Matthew alluding to? Suggestions referring to the 'watchmen' (*nōserim*) of Jer 31:6–7 who announce the good news of Israel's salvation, or to the 'princes' (*nezirim*) of Lam 4:7 are too far-fetched to be taken seriously. A more widely accepted view is that Mt 2:23 refers to the 'shoot' (*nēser*) of Isa 11:1 which is interpreted messianically in the *Targum* and in the writings of Qumran. However, in its other occurrences 'shoot' does not have any messianic connotations (Isa 14:19; 60:21; Dan 11:7). The plural 'the prophets' would suggest that Matthew alludes to other Old Testament texts as well which refer to a 'messianic shoot', but by the more usual term *semah*. However, such a multiple allusion would be understandable only in Hebrew, and would therefore be unsuitable for (at least part of) Matthew's readers.

Recently, Raymond Brown has proposed an allusion to Isa 4:3, 'he will be called holy', and Judg 16:17, 'I am a Nazirite of God' or 'I am a holy one of God'. George Soares Prabhu, on the other hand, defends an allusion to Judg 13:5, '. . . for the boy shall be a Nazirite to God from birth; and he shall begin to deliver Israel . . .'. We feel much inclined towards this last suggestion because the text is found in the *birth narrative of Samson*, and because the phrase 'he shall begin to deliver Israel' is paralleled by the 'he will save his people' of Mt 1:21. Matthew seems to have intended to refer to the Book of Judges as one of the 'earlier prophets'.

The final pericope of Mt 1 – 2 stresses that according to God's will the Messiah had to live in Nazareth (Galilee). This could have been the source of the objections to Jesus' messianic character, since most Jews believed that Judea (Bethlehem) was to be the place of origin of the Messiah. Mt 2:22–23 illustrates a striking contrast between the Matthean and Lucan infancy narratives. Luke must explain how Jesus, conceived at Nazareth, was born in Bethlehem, while Matthew must show how Jesus, born in Bethlehem, was considered in later years to be a Nazarene.

5   The Infancy Narrative of Luke

The literary form of Luke 1 – 2

We pointed out in Chapter One that the infancy narratives were not a part of the early preaching of the Church. However, on the level of the redaction of the gospel, the infancy narrative is an integral part of Luke's entire two-volume work, namely the gospel of Luke and the Acts of the Apostles. Though an integral part of Luke-Acts, the infancy narrative stands out from the rest of it in content and style. Whatever theory of literary construction is adopted, the question of the literary form remains. We have already discussed the designation *midrash* as applied to the infancy narratives. Although some feel that the term *midrash* cannot be correctly applied to Lk 1 – 2, or to any part of it, we feel that recent study on the literary form of Jewish *midrash* allows us to use it to describe the literary form of the infancy narratives. To prevent any misunderstanding, as we discussed earlier, we could speak of *Christian midrash*.

The apocalyptic character of the Lucan annunciation scenes involving Zechariah, Mary, and the shepherds has been pointed out. We should note that there is a very close relationship between *midrash* and *apocalyptic*.

Apocalyptic is a literary form in which a contemporary writer presents his message as visions and revelations allegedly given to some figure of the past. These revelations have been hidden for a long time but are now published. They give hope to people who suffer persecution and disaster by asserting that a better future lies ahead. To assure confidence in his message, the author presents events already past as being predicted by someone. Since these things have happened as predicted, the readers are encouraged to believe also what is said of events that are still to come. Apocalyptic makes frequent use of colourful imagery and mysterious symbols. It is sometimes combined with *midrash*.

The Book of Daniel is the model of all apocalypses and the infancy narrative of Luke cannot be understood correctly so long as we do not grasp its connection with the Book of Daniel and its apocalyptic themes. In his prologue (Lk 1:1–4), Luke explicitly states that he intends to write history, but it immediately strikes us that the author's treatment of the events differs entirely from that of a modern history book. Luke's history is religious historiography biblically presented, in close association with ancient biblical stories, especially as regards the annunciation narratives. The author uses certain biblical settings and traditional patterns, particularly when human means of expression fail him. The many points of contact between certain visions from the Book of Daniel and the appearances of the angel to Zechariah and Mary show that Luke is giving these passages an *apocalyptic setting*. We list the following parallels:

Luke		Daniel	
(1)	1:9–10: *the vision takes place during the sacrifice. The presence of the crowd indicates that it was the evening sacrifice.*	(1) 9:21:	at the time of the evening sacrifice.
(2)	1:12: And Zechariah was troubled. 1:29: But she was greatly troubled. 2:9: And they were filled with fear.	(2) 8:17: 10:8–9:	When he came, I was frightened. I was left alone and saw this great vision, and no strength was left in me.
(3)	1:13: But the angel said to him, 'Do not be afraid, Zechariah, for . . .' 1:30: And the angel said to her, 'Do not be afraid, Mary, for . . .' 2:10: And the angel said to them, 'Be not afraid, for . . .'	(3) 10:12: 10:19:	Then he said to me, 'Fear not, Daniel, for . . .' 'Fear not, peace be with you . . .'
(4)	1:13: 'your prayer is heard.'	(4) 10:12:	'your words have been heard . . .'

(5) 1:17: 'to turn the hearts of the fathers to the children, and the disobedient to the wisdom of the just.'

(5) 12:3: 'And those who are wise shall shine like the brightness of the firmament; and those who turn many to righteousness, like the stars for ever and ever.'

(6) 1:19: 'I am Gabriel, who stand in the presence of God.'
1:26: the angel Gabriel was sent from God.

(6) 8:16: 'Gabriel, make this man understand the vision.'
9:21: the man Gabriel whom I had seen in the vision . . . , came to me in swift flight.

(7) 1:19: 'I am Gabriel, who stand in the presence of God; and I was sent to speak to you.'

(7) 7:16: I approached one of those who stood there (*i.e. in the presence of God*).
10:11: 'give heed to the words that I speak to you, . . . for now I have been sent to you.'

(8) 1:20: 'And behold, you will be silent and unable to speak.'

(8) 10:15: When he had spoken to me according to these words, I turned my face toward the ground and was dumb.

(9) 1:28: 'Hail, full of grace (*better*: Hail, highly favoured).'

(9) 9:23: 'You are greatly beloved.'
10:11: 'O Daniel, man greatly beloved.'

(10) 1:29:	she . . . considered in her mind what sort of greeting this might be.	(10) 8:15:	When I, Daniel, had seen the vision, I sought to understand it.
		8:27:	I was appalled by the vision and did not understand it.
(11) 1:35:	'the child to be born will be called holy.'	(11) 9:24:	'to anoint a holy place (*or:* holy one).'
(12) 1:64:	And immediately his mouth was opened and his tongue loosed, and he spoke.	(12) 10:16:	And behold, one in the likeness of the sons of men touched my lips; then I opened my mouth and spoke.
(13) 2:19:	But Mary kept all these things, pondering them in her heart (*en tēi kardiai*).	(13) 7:28:	but I kept the matter in my mind (*en kardiai*).
2:51:	And his mother kept all these things in her heart (*en tēi kardiai*).		

These parallels show clearly that in Lk 1 – 2 we are dealing with apocalyptic visions, so that we can speak of an *apocalypse of Zechariah*. The annunciation to Mary belongs to the same literary form, although the parallels with Daniel are less obvious.

A further study of the context of the message, within this apocalyptic framework, leads to the discovery that both with Zechariah (Lk 1:13–17) and with Mary (Lk 1:31–33), the author keeps to the style and the layout of the annunciation narratives of the Old Testament. When in the Bible a birth is announced by an angel, the scheme, in spite of some modifications, is always the same (Gen 16:11–12; 17:19–20; Judg 13:3–5; Isa 7:14–17; Mt 1:21; Lk 1:13–17; 1:31–33). We find this scheme in its purest form in the annunciation to Hagar (Gen 16:11–12; we give here the Jerusalem Bible version, which is more closely parallel to Lk 1:31):

Then the angel of Yahweh said to her:
'Now you have conceived and you will bear a son,
and you shall name him Ishmael,
for Yahweh has heard your cries of distress.
A wild-ass of a man he will be,
against every man, and every man against him,
setting himself to defy all his brothers.'

We always find the same elements: (1) pregnancy, (2) birth, (3) giving of the name, (4) the future of the child. In fact the scheme which we find in Genesis and all the other passages mentioned is the natural one. We should understand the text of Luke in the light of these Old Testament annunciations. In both annunciation narratives in Luke (of John and of Jesus) we find the same basic scheme, though we must pay attention to certain differences, which will be pointed out in the exegesis.

Let us now indicate the scheme of Luke's annunciation narratives:

The Annunciations of the Birth of John and Jesus
(Lk 1:13–17 and 1:31–33)

	John	Jesus
(1)	pregnancy: *not explicitly mentioned*	you will conceive in your womb (Lk 1:31)
(2)	birth: your wife Elizabeth will bear you a son (Lk 1:13)	and bear a son (Lk 1:31)
(3)	giving of the name: and you shall call his name John (Lk 1:13).	and you shall call his name Jesus (Lk 1:31).
(4)	future of the child: . . . for he will be great before the Lord . . . (Lk 1:14–17).	He will be great, and will be called the Son of the Most High . . . (Lk 1:32–33).

In addition to the style and the layout of the classical annunciation narratives, we find elements in Lk 1 that are characteristic of the fixed pattern of the narratives of Old Testament *vocations* or *calls*. The same scheme occurs regularly:

(1) Yahweh's call and mission;
(2) objection by the person called;

(3) objection overruled by a promise;
(4) a sign in confirmation of the promise (given or requested).

Let us take an example, the call of Gideon in Judg 6:

(1) Yahweh's call and mission: 'Go in this might of yours and deliver Israel from the hand of Midian; do not I send you?' (Judg 6:14).
(2) Gideon's objection: 'Pray, Lord, how can I deliver Israel?' (Judg 6:15).
(3) Refutation of the objection and promise: 'I will be with you and you shall smite the Midianites as one man' (Judg 6:16).
(4) Sign of confirmation requested by Gideon: 'If now I have found favour with you, then show me a sign that it is you who speak with me . . .' (Judg 6:17–18).

The same scheme occurs in the call of Moses (Ex 3:10–12; two signs are given in Ex 4:3–9) and Jeremiah (Jer 1:4–12). In each of these narratives there is a stereotyped recurrence of the request for a sign. This sign does not serve as an authentication of the apparition, since Gideon and Moses are well aware that it is Yahweh who speaks; it serves rather as a confirmation of the mission. The Old Testament sees nothing reprehensible in the request for such sign; it is not an expression of disbelief and it is frequently given by Yahweh or his prophets (see I Sam 2:34; 10:1; Isa 37:30; 38:7; Jer 44:29). The sign is sometimes even requested (Judg 6:17, 36; II Kgs 20:8) and in Isa 7:11 the prophet himself invites Ahaz to ask for it. The content of the sign is not necessarily connected with the principal prophecy, but its role is nevertheless to serve the latter. These data are especially valuable for explaining the apparitions in Lk 1, which closely follow the pattern of *vocation* or *call* narratives.

The Calls of Zechariah and of Mary
(Lk 1:13–20 and 1:31–36)

	Zechariah	Mary
(1)	Yahweh's call and mission: *This is contained in the annunciation of the birth of John the Baptist (Lk 1:13–17).*	*This is contained in the annunciation of the birth of Jesus (Lk 1:31–33).*
(2)	objection: How shall I know this? For I am an old man, and my wife is advanced in years (Lk 1:18).	How can this be, since I have no husband? (Lk 1:34).

(3)   refutation of the objection:
I am Gabriel . . . and I was
sent to speak to you, and to
bring you this good news
(Lk 1:19).

The Holy Spirit will come
upon you, and the power of the
Most High will overshadow
you . . . (Lk 1:35).

(4)   sign of confirmation:
And behold, you will be
silent and unable to
speak until the day that
these things come to
pass (Lk 1:20).

And behold, your kinswoman
Elizabeth in her old age has
also conceived . . . (Lk 1:36).

The apocalyptic setting and the striking parallel with the pattern of the Old Testament narratives of *annunciations* and *calls* should not lead to exaggerated conclusions. The similarities are mainly confined to literary form. It is improbable that the angel himself was bound to a definite pattern; it is rather the evangelist who conformed to traditional, biblical patterns. Present-day study of the gospels shows that the evangelists take considerable freedom in phrasing the gospel message, even in those instances where they must have been capable of an accurate historical reproduction of the events they narrated. The considerations above make it clear to what extent certain pericopes and details of Lk 1 – 2 are inspired by Old Testament passages.

Throughout the infancy narrative, even more than in the rest of his gospel, Luke is concerned, not with the facts only but, in a special way, with the *meaning* of the facts. Moreover, the author was apparently not in possession of accurate historical details regarding certain events, especially the annunciations; because of the nature of these events he was no doubt compelled to 'flesh out' his narrative, and the ancient biblical narratives provided the material needed.

It is clear then that Luke's method of writing does not allow a simple, unqualified answer to the question: What actually happened? There is not the slightest doubt that there are a number of basically historical facts behind Lk 1 – 2. But what are we to say of the apparitions of the angel Gabriel to Zechariah and Mary? Did he really appear to them? We would not *a priori* exclude the possibility of an apparition. But it is more likely that Luke has expressed himself in traditional and hallowed images of his times.

Thus he tells us that Zechariah was made to understand that Elizabeth would give birth to a remarkable son. And Mary was called to play a very important role in God's plan of salvation. She was to be the mother of the Messiah. The essential factor is that both Zechariah and Mary knew themselves to be called by God. The manner in which God's will was made known to them is secondary. If this is our assessment of the annunciation to Zechariah and Mary, we should say the same of the angel's announcement to the shepherds. The canticles, *Magnificat, Benedictus, Nunc Dimittis*, and the canticle of the angels, are intended to express the spiritual meaning of the events narrated.

Luke is convinced that Jesus' birth has been prepared by God. It forms the climax and fulfilment of the promise made to Abraham and proclaimed in many different ways by the prophets. In this spirit the evangelist has elaborated and developed his narration. Using God's preparatory words and works in the Old Testament, Lk 1 – 2 becomes a meditation and elucidation of new developments in the history of salvation.

Without disputing the results of the previous studies, some commentators remind us that we should also take into account the New Testament background of Luke's narrative. The revelation of Jesus' birth to the shepherds (Lk 2:8–20) could belong to the literary form not so much of Old Testament angelic annunciations, but rather of New Testament apostolic preaching. The vocabulary employed certainly echoes that of imperial proclamations and bears some resemblances to Acts 2:36; 9:22, etc. Luke's intention could be to show how the word of salvation preached by the earliest missionaries is a message from heaven. Not only the theological themes but also the structure and the literary form of the narratives are deeply rooted in the rest of the New Testament. Luke very likely wrote it with the apostolic activity of Christian missionaries in mind. To him, the annunciation of the birth of the Saviour may well have been a way of prefiguring the missionary preaching of Christian salvation. Therefore, Luke may be describing the episode at Bethlehem in vocabulary inspired by the apostolic preaching of his day.

The structure of the Lucan infancy narrative

According to many scholars, Luke's infancy narrative is composed in the form of a diptych which has two phases:

(i)   before the births of John and Jesus (Lk 1:5–38), and
(ii) the accounts of the births of John and Jesus (Lk 1:57 – 2:40).

Each of these phases has a complementary episode: the visitation (Lk 1:39–56) in the first case, and the finding of Jesus in the Temple (Lk 2:41–52) in the second case.

(i)   Diptych of annunciations (Lk 1:5–56)

(1) Annunciation of John's birth (Lk 1:5–25): introduction of the parents apparition of the angel	(2) Annunciation of Jesus' birth (Lk 1:26–38): introduction of the parents entry of the angel

Zechariah is troubled	Mary is troubled
'Fear not . . .'	'Fear not . . .'
annunciation of the birth	annunciation of the birth
Q. 'How shall I know this?'	Q. 'How can this be?'
A. Reprimand by the angel	A. Revelation by the angel
constrained silence of Zechariah	spontaneous reply of Mary
departure of Zechariah	departure of the angel

        (3) Complementary episode: visitation (Lk 1:39–56):
                canticle: *Magnificat*
                conclusion: return of Mary

(ii) Diptych of births (Lk 1:57 – 2:52)

(4) Birth of John (Lk 1:57–58): (5) Birth of Jesus (Lk 2:1–20):
joy at the birth | joy at the birth
(with canticle element) | canticle of the angels
Circumcision and manifestation of John (Lk 1:59–79): (6) Circumcision and manifestation of Jesus (Lk 2:21–35):

manifestation of the prophet | manifestation of the Saviour

canticle: *Benedictus* | canticle: *Nunc Dimittis*
 | Supplementary episode: Anna (Lk 2:36–38)
conclusion: refrain of growth (Lk 1:80) | conclusion: refrain of growth (Lk 2:40)

        (7) Complementary episode: finding in the Temple (Lk 2:41–52)
                refrain of growth (Lk 2:52)

Three verses recur by way of chorus and obviously have a part to play in the overall construction. Scholars call them *literary seams*. They indicate the main joints of the narrative, mark the transition from one scene to the next and bind the whole into a closely-knit composition. These three literary seams are the *leave-taking* (Lk 1:23; 1:38; 1:56; 2:20; 2:39; 2:51), the *growing-up* (Lk 1:80; 2:40; 2:52), and the *treasuring* (Lk 2:19; 2:51).

From this plan it appears that John and Jesus are compared and constrasted, but the greatness of Jesus is emphasized. Mary is superior to Zechariah and, more explicitly, her son by far surpasses the son of Zechariah. The central scene is clearly the birth of Jesus and, more precisely, the annunciation to the shepherds.

The texts dealing with John the Baptist and those dealing with Jesus are closely related, for the texts dealing with John acquire a Christian meaning which they could not originally have had by themselves. The texts about John, as Luke found them, most likely already formed a unified whole in a Christian or pre-Christian tradition. This unit or block had been, according to the methods of *midrash*, patterned after the stories of Samuel (I Sam 1 – 3), while undergoing some influence also from the story of Samson's birth (Judg 13).

Central to the present structure of Lk 1 – 2 is the parallelism between John and Jesus. There are two annunciations (Lk 1:5–25; 1:26–38); two conceptions (Lk 1:24–25; 1:35); two births (Lk 1:57–58; 2:6–7); two circumcisions (Lk 1:59; 2:21); and two concluding summaries of each child's early years (Lk 1:80; 2:52; see also 2:40). This symmetry becomes the basis of the contrast between John and Jesus, and a means of emphasizing the superiority of Jesus in all respects.

6 The Annunciation Narratives

(Exegesis of Lk 1:5–56)

Luke introduces his book with a prologue or preface (Lk 1:1–4). This follows the type of introduction generally used by Greek writers of the period. In a long and carefully constructed sentence, he speaks of the contents, the sources, the method, and the purpose of his work, and of the occasion which gave rise to it. This prologue does not really belong to the infancy narrative, but introduces the whole of the gospel as well as the Acts of the Apostles where the introductory verse (Acts 1:1) recalls this prologue of the gospel.

Annunciation of the birth of John (Lk 1:5–25)

Lk 1:5–25 is a self-contained story which may be divided into three parts:

(1) Lk 1:5–7:   introduction of the dramatis personae.
(2) Lk 1:8–23:   annunciation of conception to Zechariah:
                    8–10: setting;
                    11–20: core;
                    21–23: conclusion.
(3) Lk 1:24–25:   epilogue: Elizabeth's pregnancy and her praise of God.

> **Verses 5–7:** (It came to pass) in the days of Herod, king of Judea, there was a priest named Zechariah, of the division of Abijah; and he had a wife of the daughters of Aaron, and her name was Elizabeth. (6) And they were both righteous before God, walking in all the commandments and ordinances of the Lord blameless. (7) But they had no child, because Elizabeth was barren, and both were advanced in years.

The RSV omits the initial words 'It came to pass'. This phrase is used in a related formal structure at Lk 2:1, 'Now it came to pass (again omitted by RSV) in those days a decree went out from Caesar Augustus'. Two sets of data are distinguished: Lk 1 introduces John and Jesus to the reader; Lk 2 focuses attention on the person and mission of Jesus apart from any reference to John.

Zechariah was a priest 'of the division of Abijah'. The priests were divided into twenty-four sections which contributed in succession a week's service at the Temple. Thus each section would serve twice a year. Elizabeth was of the tribe of Aaron and therefore shared the priestly ancestry of Zechariah. Both qualify genealogically for the parentage of John the Baptist.

They also qualify morally: 'they were both righteous before God'. This is explained in the next clause: 'walking in all the commandments and ordinances of the Lord blameless'.

> Combining priestly origins and blameless observance of the Law, Zechariah and Elizabeth were for Luke the representatives of the best in the religion of Israel; and as a remnant which received the 'good news' (1:19), they personified the continuity in salvation history.[19]

Elizabeth was barren (literally: sterile) like Sarah (Gen 16:1ff.), Rebekah (Gen 25:21), Rachel (Gen 30:22), the mother of Samson (Judg 13:2), and Hannah the mother of Samuel (I Sam 1 – 2). Also, like Abraham and Sarah, she and her husband were 'advanced in years' and so, humanly speaking, would remain childless. Hence the child to be born is in a special way the *gift of God*, a child of grace like Isaac, Samson, and Samuel.

> **Verses 8–10:** Now while he was serving as priest before God when his division was on duty, (9) according to the custom of the priesthood, it fell to him by lot to enter the temple of the Lord and burn incense. (10) And the whole multitude of the people were praying outside at the hour of incense.

The gospel begins in Jerusalem, at the Temple, where it will also end (cf. Lk 24:52–53, 'And they worshipped him, and returned to Jerusalem with great joy, and were continually in the temple blessing God'). The time of Jesus is centred on Jerusalem, and more precisely on the Temple.

Since there were large numbers of priests and Levites, it was determined by lot who would serve in the Temple at a particular time. To burn incense in the Temple was a great privilege, and we may suppose that Zechariah considered it the crowning experience of his life as a priest. Though there was an offering both morning and evening, the presence of the multitude in the outer courts suggests the evening offering (compare Dan 9:21).

'The whole multitude of the people were praying outside': Luke repeatedly associates prayer with important moments in the gospel (see Lk 3:21; 5:16; 6:12; 9:18, 28; 22:41). The reader is constantly reminded of the divine dimension of the events. Like Daniel (see Dan 9:20ff.), Zechariah is going to be subjected to an apocalyptic experience.

Verses 11–12: And there appeared to him an angel of the Lord standing on the right side of the altar of incense. (12) And Zechariah was troubled when he saw him, and fear fell upon him.

The Old Testament usually calls attention to God's presence by describing the reaction of the persons involved. To be 'troubled' and subject to 'fear' is a typical reaction to divine manifestation or apocalyptic events (see Dan 7:28).

Verse 13: But the angel said to him, 'Do not be afraid, Zechariah, for your prayer is heard, and your wife Elizabeth will bear you a son, and you shall call his name John.'

The phrase 'Do not be afraid' recurs repeatedly in the gospel (see Lk 1:30; 2:10; 5:10; 8:50; 12:32) and is reminiscent of similar phrases in the Old Testament (Gen 15:1; Isa 7:4; Dan 10:12). Its use here indicates that the time of God's intervention on behalf of his people has arrived. Zechariah has prayed for a son, and his request is about to be granted: 'your prayer is heard' (compare Dan 10:12, 'your words have been heard').

As was already said in the previous chapter, Lk 1:13–17 follows the style and outline of the annunciation narratives of the Old Testament. These always comprise the same elements: (1) pregnancy, (2) birth, (3) the naming of the child, and (4) the announcement of its future. The second and third elements of this pattern are found in Lk 1:13, the fourth element is developed in Lk 1:14–17. The annunciation of John's birth, communicated to the father (as also in Gen 17:19 and in Mt 1:21), does not mention the first element, the pregnancy. This is no sufficient reason, however, to think that Elizabeth's pregnancy has already begun at the time of the vision. Lk 1:24 says: 'After these days his wife Elizabeth conceived', and according to the style of these narratives this can only mean that the barren wife became pregnant after the vision. The announcement concerns a reality which will be realized in the near future (see I Sam 1:19–20 and Judg 13:24).

The announcement of the pregnancy and birth is normally followed by the indication of the child's name, here 'you shall call his name John', and a phrase giving the reason for the choice of this name is often added. This latter element, at least in its usual form, is lacking in this case. It is, however, possible that we might see a modified version of it in Lk 1:13. The words 'for your prayer is heard' probably allude to the Hebrew equivalent of *John*, namely *Jochanan*, which means 'God is merciful' and recalls the word from the same root *chanan* meaning 'prayer'. There may therefore be a relationship between the name *John* and the reason for the choice of the name, namely that God has heard Zechariah's prayer.

> **Verses 14–17:** 'And you will have joy and gladness, and many will rejoice at his birth;
> (15) for he will be great before the Lord, and he shall drink no wine nor strong drink, and he will be filled with the Holy Spirit, even from his mother's womb.
> (16) And he will turn many of the sons of Israel to the Lord their God,
> (17) and he will go before him in the spirit and power of Elijah, to turn the hearts of the fathers to the children, and the disobedient to the wisdom of the just, to make ready for the Lord a people prepared.'

Note first the stress given to 'joy': 'and you will have joy and gladness, and many will rejoice'. Joy is the keynote of the messianic age and is specially emphasized by Luke (see Lk 2:10; 15:6–10; 24:52; Acts 8:8; 13:52). This joy will not be limited to Zechariah and Elizabeth, but will be shared by 'many' in Israel. 'Many' is probably a Semitic expression for the totality of the people of Israel. God's invitation knows no limitations.

Here we have the fourth element of the annunciation pattern: the future of the child. It is obvious that the description of the child's future goes beyond the individual viewpoint. Thus, in the case of Ishmael (Gen 16:12; 17:20) and of Isaac (Gen 17:19, 21) the future of the whole people is foretold. In Judg 13:5b, Samson receives the mission to begin the deliverance of Israel. The prediction of the child's future very often includes a charge, a mission. In Lk 1:15–17 this element is given special emphasis.

John 'will be great before the Lord'. Compare and contrast this with Lk 1:32, 'He will be great, and will be called the Son of the Most High'. This statement also echoes Lk 7:28, 'Among those born of women none is greater than John'. Verse 15b is a combination of Num 6:3, 'he shall separate himself from wine and strong drink', and Judg 13:4, 'Therefore beware, and drink no wine or strong drink'. This would appear to indicate that John lived as a *Nazirite*. Like the *Nazirites* and *Rechabites*, two groups of ascetics in contemporary Judaism, John will abstain from strong drink, 'and he will be filled with the Holy Spirit'. A certain contrast between strong drink and the Holy Spirit is probably to be felt, as expressed, for example, in Eph 5:18,

'And do not get drunk with wine, for that is debauchery; but be filled with the Spirit'.

In Lk 1:16–17, John is described as the *New Elijah* in wording borrowed from the prophet Malachi: 'He walked with me in peace and uprightness, and he turned many from iniquity' (Mal 2:6); 'Behold, I send my messenger to prepare the way before me' (Mal 3:1); 'Behold, I will send you Elijah the prophet before the great and terrible day of the Lord comes (Mal 4:5[3:23 in Hebrew text]); 'And he will turn the hearts of fathers to their children and the hearts of children to their fathers' (Mal 4:6 [3:24]). Whereas the text of Malachi says that the mission of Elijah consists in restoring peace in families, in Sir 48:10 the restoration of Israel is added: 'to turn the heart of the father to the son, and to restore the tribes of Jacob'. Compare with this the last part of Lk 1:17, 'to make ready for the Lord a people prepared'.

This identification of John with the new Elijah is familiar from the gospels of Mark and Matthew. We should, however, pay attention to the fact that in Lk 1:16–17, John is indicated not as the forerunner of the Messiah, but as the forerunner of Yahweh himself, as in Malachi. The 'Lord' of Lk 1:17 is the same as the 'Lord their God' in Lk 1:16. Jesus the Messiah seems to be absent from this picture of John the Baptist. It is Yahweh himself who will intervene and John, the eschatological prophet, is his forerunner. Consequently some scholars think that this narrative comes from the circle of John's own disciples, who did not intend to stress the inferiority of the prophet with regard to Jesus the Messiah. It is Luke's redaction that brings out this comparison and contrast, but even here the texts about John the Baptist may still reveal their previous origin.

However, the parallelism between the visions of Zechariah and Mary is not limited to the annunciations proper. Both react to the annunciation by asking a question. Luke has used another Old Testament pattern, the scheme of the narratives of calls in the Old Testament. This pattern, we recall, is composed of four elements: (1) Yahweh's call and mission; (2) question or objection by the person called; (3) the objection overruled by a promise; (4) a sign in confirmation of the promise (given or requested).

The first element, the call and mission, is contained in the annunciation: the annunciation of the birth of John the Baptist implies a mission and call for Zechariah. In the following verses, we find the other elements of the pattern.

Verses 18–20: And Zechariah said to the angel, 'How shall I know this? For I am an old man, and my wife is advanced in years.' (19) And the angel answered him, 'I am Gabriel, who stand in the presence of God; and I was sent to speak to you, and to bring you this good news. (20) And behold, you will be silent and unable to speak until the day that these things come to pass, because you did not believe my words, which will be fulfilled in their time.'

Here the parallelism between Zechariah and Mary seems to become antithetical. Zechariah asks for a sign and is punished for his lack of faith (Lk 1:20). Mary, on the contrary, is called blessed because of her faith (Lk 1:45). She asks only for an explanation of what she does not understand.

This traditional exegesis, however, leaves room for doubt and some questioning. In Gen 15:8 Abraham replies to the promise of Yahweh with the same question: 'O Lord God, how am I to know that I shall possess it?' This question occurs in a context in which Abraham's faith is stressed: 'And he (Abraham) believed the Lord; and he reckoned it to him as righteousness' (Gen 15:6). In the story of Genesis, Abraham's question does not seem to be out of place and is certainly not understood as a lack of faith. Abraham never hesitates to express his objections (see Gen 15:1–5, 7–16; 17:1–21; 18:10–14). The same is found in a more developed form in the other *vocation* stories in the Old Testament, as was shown earlier in the discussion of the form of Lk 1 – 2. These data from Genesis are especially instructive for explaining the visions in Lk 1, which follow strictly the stereotyped scheme of the Old Testament *calls*.

Because the Old Testament does not find anything reprehensible in the demand for a sign, we are less ready to think that Mary's faith would exclude such a request (see later under Lk 1:34–36). In the case of Zechariah we also find a question and an implied demand for a sign. The angel refutes the objection by an appeal to his mission (Lk 1:19) and grants the sign: Zechariah will be dumb (Lk 1:20). This sign will be realized immediately after the vision (Lk 1:22).

We face here a strange fact: the dumbness is both a sign and a *punishment* because, as the text says, he did not believe (Lk 1:20). In view of what we have said about the pattern of the Old Testament *calls*, which is followed by Luke here, this is unexpected. Similar requests are never understood as lack of faith! The previous description of Zechariah as 'righteous before God, walking in all the commandments and ordinances of the Lord blameless' (Lk 1:6) also hardly prepares us for such a punishment! However, the theme of the seer's incapability to speak is a well-known apocalyptic feature (see Dan 10:15). This is confirmed in the further development of the narrative, where we are told that the people, realizing that Zechariah cannot speak, automatically concluded that he must have had a vision (see Lk 1:22). Finally, especially if we accept that this story already existed before its inclusion in the infancy narrative of Luke, it is hard to see how the father of the prophet could be described as lacking faith.

The present interpretation becomes understandable only on the level of Luke's redaction, because of the intended antithetical parallelism between John and Jesus on the one hand, and Mary and Zechariah on the other. Originally, Zechariah's dumbness must simply have been a sign confirming the mission given to him. A Hellenistic Christian writer (Luke himself?), knowing that Jesus during his public ministry rejected the Jews who asked for a sign, and no longer sensitive to the typically Jewish or apocalyptic character of Zechariah's vision and the features typical of this style, would certainly be tempted to interpret this dumbness in a moral sense, as punishment for lack of faith. This connotation of punishment for lack of faith may then have been added to the original story on its translation from Hebrew into Greek.

> **Verses 21–23:** And the people were waiting for Zechariah, and they wondered at his delay in the temple. (22) And when he came out, he could not speak to them, and they perceived that he had seen a vision in the temple; and he made signs to them and remained dumb. (23) And when his time of service was ended, he went to his home.

The incense offering was a simple and brief ceremony. Since Zechariah lingered longer than was customary, the people, who awaited the priestly blessing (see Num 6:24–26), 'wondered'. When they noticed that he was unable to speak they concluded that he had seen a vision, for dumbness was an accepted consequence of apocalyptic experience (see Dan 10:15–17).

The departure of Zechariah (Lk 1:23) indicates the end of the episode. As we saw in the discussion of the structure of Lk 1 – 2, Luke frequently indicates the end of an episode by saying that one or more of the persons involved in the scene leaves. This we call a *seam* of *leave-taking* (see Lk 1:38; 1:56; 2:20; 2:39; 2:51).

> **Verses 24–25:** After these days his wife Elizabeth conceived, and for five months she hid herself, saying (25) 'Thus the Lord has done to me in the days when he looked on me, to take away my reproach among men.'

His wife Elizabeth conceived. Luke undoubtedly intends to say that John was conceived in the normal way, but at the same time he wants to stress that it was due to a special intervention of God that he was conceived despite old age and barrenness. Why Elizabeth should have hidden herself for five months, that is, concealed her pregnancy, is not at once clear. No such custom at the time seems to be known. Perhaps the explanation is to be sought in the necessities of the narrative. The pregnancy of Elizabeth is to be first announced by the angel to Mary in the 'sixth' month. Elizabeth's hiding will then explain why the news of her pregnancy has not yet reached her young relative before the angel's mission to Nazareth. It is not to be known before that time so that Elizabeth's pregnancy may serve as a sign from the angel for Mary (Lk 1:36).

Like so many holy women in the Old Testament, Elizabeth praises God because he has taken away her reproach, that is, the shame of childlessness. We could refer here to Gen 30:22–23: 'Then God remembered Rachel, and God hearkened to her and opened her womb. She conceived and bore a son, and said, God has taken away my reproach.'

Annunciation of the birth of Jesus (Lk 1:26–38)

The close parallelism between this and the foregoing section is clear from the plan given earlier in Chapter Five. Both narratives are presented in a characteristic literary form to which Luke has faithfully conformed. This is clear from a comparison with the Old Testament *call narratives* discussed above in connection with the annunciation of John's birth.

Recently, however, it has been pointed out that this parallelism may not be so perfect as is often thought. Some important elements in Lk 1:26–38 have no counterpart in Lk 1:5–25, and even where the formulations are very similar, the meaning is nevertheless repeatedly somewhat different, because of the contrast between a 'horizontal hagiographic code' for Lk 1:5–25 and a 'vertical code of revelation' for Lk 1:26–38: John 'will be great before the Lord', but Jesus 'will be called the Son of the Most High'. Under rather similar appearances and notwithstanding their identical structure, the two annunciations are seen to reveal different orientations.[20]

The apocalyptic character of the annunciation narrative has also been stressed. It is clear the annunciation does not belong to the apocalyptic literary genre, but nevertheless the narrative has certain features of apocalyptic literature. A revelation is mediated by a celestial being to a human addressee to unveil a transcendent reality which nevertheless belongs to time and space. The annunciation follows an apocalyptic thought pattern. The viewpoint is eschatological; in the final analysis, the annunciation intends to relate an apocalyptic event. Beyond the narrative of the annunciation and the miraculous conception, the text intends to make of the angelic announcement the primordial revelation that the child about to be born is the fulfilment of the promises and the eschatological manifestation of God's power.[21]

Lk 1:26–38 has a certain formal balance. Its symmetrical arrangement is evident, though not perfect: elements C and F have no counterpart, and the elements of the two parts of the angel's message do not appear in the same order:

| (1) | Mission of the messenger | 1:26 | A |
| (2) | The addressee | 1:27 | B |

(3)	Greeting	1:28	C
(4)	First reaction	1:29	D
(5)	First part of the message		E
	'you have found favour'	1:30	E a
	'you will conceive'	1:31	E b
	first description	1:32–33	E c
(6)	Second reaction	1:34	D'
(7)	Second part of the message		E'
	'The Holy Spirit will come'	1:35a	E'a'
	second description	1:35b	E'c'
	'Elizabeth has also conceived'	1:36	E'b'
	'nothing will be impossible'	1:37	F
(8)	Answer of Mary	1:38a	B'
(9)	Departure of the angel	1:38b	A'

Verses 26–27: In the sixth month the angel Gabriel was sent from God to a city of Galilee named Nazareth, (27) to a virgin betrothed to a man whose name was Joseph, of the house of David; and the virgin's name was Mary.

'In the sixth month' of Elizabeth's pregnancy 'the angel Gabriel' who had already appeared to Zechariah, just as he appeared to Daniel, 'was sent from God . . . to a virgin' whose 'name was Mary'. It is worth noting that these are the only three passages in the Bible where Gabriel is mentioned. Throughout the infancy narrative of Luke the interest centres on Mary. This is in striking contrast to Matthew, where the angel (whose name is not mentioned) appears to Joseph, who remains the principal actor throughout the narrative.

The angel Gabriel was sent to a 'virgin': the Greek word *parthenos* meant a young girl of marriageable age. As we will see in Lk 1:34–35, Luke holds that Mary is a virgin in the strict sense of the word, but he does not emphasize this here. Mary was betrothed: in contrast to engagement nowadays, betrothal was, in contemporary Jewish law, a binding contract. But it was not until a year after the espousals that the bridegroom would take the bride to his home and they would live as husband and wife (cf. Mt 1:24).

Joseph was 'of the house of David', and so the legal Davidic descent of Jesus was assured. The phrase 'the house of David' may already be an allusion to the 'Covenant with David' in II Samuel, where we read of God's promise, 'the Lord will make you a house' (II Sam 7:11). The close relationship with this text becomes obvious in Lk 1:32–33: 'He will be great, and will be called the Son of the Most High; and the Lord God will give him the throne of his father David, and he will reign over the house of Jacob forever; and of his kingdom there will be no end'. This is a direct echo of II Sam 7:7–16, especially 7:9, 12–16: '. . . and I will make for you a great name. . . . I will raise up your offspring after you, who shall come forth from your body, and I will establish his kingdom. He shall build a house for my name, and I will establish the throne of his kingdom for ever. I will be his father, and he shall be my son . . . your throne shall be established for ever.'

> **Verses 28–30:** And he came to her and said, 'Hail, full of grace (*better*: highly favoured), the Lord is with you!' (29) But she was greatly troubled at the saying, and considered in her mind what sort of greeting this might be. (30) And the angel said to her, 'Do not be afraid, Mary, for you have found favour with God.'

The address 'Hail' is equivalent to 'Greetings' but conveys also the sense of rejoicing. Probably, Luke had a specific Old Testament passage in mind: Zeph 3:14–17, 'Sing aloud, O daughter of Zion; shout, O Israel! Rejoice and exult with all your heart, O daughter of Jerusalem! . . .'. Compare Joel 2:21–27 and Zech 9:9–10. 'Rejoice' (*chaire*) is found in these three texts and nowhere else in the Septuagint, except Lam 4:21. Therefore in Lk 1:28 we may also have the same meaning: an invitation to rejoice at the advent of the messianic times.

The translation 'favoured one', or 'highly favoured', given in a footnote and preferred by the Jerusalem Bible, is preferable to 'full of grace'. The salutation announces the gracious attitude of the Lord toward Mary, the 'favoured' one. As is the case elsewhere (Lk 1:38, 48), Mary is described as receiving grace, not as endowed with the power to give grace.

We return here to the call of Gideon (Judg 6:12–18) which we referred to as a clear example of one of the literary patterns which Luke followed. The close parallel between Judg 6:12, 'The Lord is with you, you mighty man of valour', and Lk 1:28 indicates that the address by Gabriel, *kecharitōmenē*, cannot be just a conventional greeting. Neither can it be understood as a reference to Mary's personal holiness. Gideon is addressed as 'mighty man of valour', a title which is a pledge of future victory for the people of Israel. He is called a hero, not because he is one, but because God is going to make him one. Similarly, in Mary's case the address does not express Mary's personal holiness and virtues which would make her a worthy recipient of the role she is going to receive, but tells us that God is going to make her a worthy instrument to execute his plans. By the phrase *kecharitōmenē* Gabriel announces that Mary has been chosen to play an important role in God's plan. Therefore, 'highly favoured one' is to be preferred to 'full of grace'. Once we have realized this, the clause 'the Lord is with you' (compare Judg 6:16, 'I will be with you') is also given its full meaning. The phrase 'highly favoured one' designates the new task Mary has been assigned by God. The assurance that the Lord will be with her is then a guarantee that the plans God has for Mary will be effectively realized.

We should recall here that Daniel is also repeatedly referred to as a man 'greatly beloved' (Dan 9:23; 10:11, 19). This connection with the Book of Daniel reminds us of the apocalyptic character or form of Gabriel's greeting.

Mary was 'greatly troubled' (compare Lk 1:12, 'Zechariah was troubled') just as Daniel was (Dan 8:17). The language is that of an apocalyptic narrative. But in Mary's case, it is not the *vision* as such but rather the *saying* that disturbs her. She asked herself 'what sort of greeting this might be', that is, what this greeting might mean. As in the case of Zechariah (Lk 1:13) and Daniel (Dan 10:12), Mary is told: 'Do not be afraid'. A similar expression is also found in Zeph 3:16: 'Do not fear, O Zion'.

'You have found favour with God' is a Semitic expression also found in Gen 6:8: 'But Noah found favour in the eyes of the Lord'. The meaning is that God is about to shower on Mary special gifts in view of the mission and task she will have to fulfil.

> **Verses 31–33:** 'And behold, you will conceive in your womb and bear a son, and you shall call his name Jesus. (32) He will be great, and will be called the Son of the Most High; and the Lord will give to him the throne of his father David, (33) and he will reign over the house of Jacob for ever; and of his kingdom there will be no end.'

As has already been pointed out, Lk 1:31–33, like Lk 1:13–17, follows the style and outline of the annunciation narratives of the Old Testament and has the same four elements:

(1)   pregnancy: 'you will conceive in your womb' (Lk 1:31);
(2)   birth: 'and bear a son' (Lk 1:31);
(3)   name-giving: 'and you shall call his name Jesus' (Lk 1:31);
(4)   future of the child: 'He will be great . . .' (Lk 1:32–33).

'Jesus' is equivalent to the name *Joshua*, which means 'God saves' (see Lk 2:11). The name reminds us of Zeph 3:17: 'The Lord, your God, is in your midst, a warrior who gives victory . . .'.

Like John (see Lk 1:15), Jesus 'will be great', but there the parallelism ends, for Jesus 'will be called the Son of the Most High'. The passive 'will be called' refers to God's action, and means: God will call him. When God calls somebody by a new name, it is more than just a name-giving. It means that God *makes* this person what he *calls* him. Therefore we should read: God will make him Son of the Most High. In the Old Testament 'Most High' often designates God. The phrase 'Son of the Most High' does not here refer to what later credal formulas mean by 'Son of God' (the second Person of the Trinity). Rather it is a messianic statement in line with II Sam 7:13–16, especially 7:14: 'I will be his father, and he shall be my son'. And there will be 'no end' to his reign (see II Sam 7:13). These verses suggest that the greatness of Jesus is of a kind which surpasses mere human greatness. These phrases also remind us of the royal psalms, especially Ps 2:7, 'You are my son, today I have begotten you', which Luke applies to Jesus in Lk 3:22, and Ps 89(88):29, 'I will establish his line for ever and his throne as the days of the heavens'.

A study of the vocabulary of Lk 1:32–33 shows that of the thirteen terms and expressions found in these verses, only one is Lucan, though not exclusively, namely 'the Most High'. Four terms are non-Lucan, while the rest are not used more frequently in Luke than elsewhere in the New Testament. As far as the theology of the passage is concerned, some have concluded that Lk 1:32–33 represents Luke's theology and is, therefore, a Lucan composition. Others, on the basis of a study of the development of Davidic messianism in Judaism previous to or contemporary with the New Testament, starting especially with the post-exilic period, and its continuity/discontinuity in Jesus' ministry and in the early Church, conclude that the theme is older than Rom 1:3–4. It is found in texts belonging to the hymn or acclamation genre, for instance, the acclamation of Jesus during his entry into Jerusalem (Lk 19:35–38), the canticle of Zechariah (Lk 1:69, 78–79), three texts in Revelation (3:7; 5:5; 22:16), and the collection of texts which introduces the argumentation of Jesus' superiority in Heb 1:5–14. Lk 1:32–33 is said to be related to this ancient current of Christology. It seems to take up a statement of the early Christian Palestinian community concerning Jesus, son of David and Son of God. By itself it constitutes an integral Christological statement, expressing the essential elements of the mystery of Christ.

Luke has also used again the other Old Testament pattern or layout of the narratives of Old Testament *calls*. As we said before, this pattern is composed of four elements:

(1)   Yahweh's call and mission;
(2)   question or objection by the person called;
(3)   the objection is overruled by a promise;
(4)   a sign of confirmation of the promise.

The first element of this pattern, the call and mission, is contained in the annunciation. Mary is called to become the mother of the Messiah in the near future. In the following verses, then, we have the other elements of the pattern.

Verses 34–37: And Mary said to the angel, 'How can this be, since I have no husband?' (35) And the angel said to her,

'The Holy Spirit will come upon you, and the power of the Most High will overshadow you; therefore the child to be born will be called holy, the Son of God. (36) And behold, your kinswoman Elizabeth in her old age has also conceived a son; and this is the sixth month with her who was called barren. (37) For with God nothing will be impossible.'

Here we have the second, third, and fourth elements of the typical pattern of the Old Testament *calls*. Mary is only a fiancée and has no intercourse with a man. Therefore she *objects* to the call and mission implied in the annunciation of the birth of Jesus: 'How can this be, since I have no husband?' One should not be mistaken about this 'how'. In this context it does not mean *in what way*, as if Mary were asking for an explanation of the way in which it is to happen. Mary is not merely asking for further information. She is in fact objecting: This is impossible in my present condition.

This also explains then why the angel concludes his refutation of the objection with the words: 'For with God nothing will be impossible' (Lk 1:37), which clearly suggests that Mary's words implied a reference to the impossibility of the whole thing. In the same way, Moses indicated the impossibility of his vocation, objecting that he was a very poor speaker: 'How then shall Pharaoh listen to me, who am a man of uncircumcised lips? (= a poor speaker)' (Ex 6:12). And Abraham objected to the promise of Yahweh by a similar question: 'O Lord God, how am I to know that I shall possess it?' (Gen 15:8). This question-objection is found in a context in which Abraham is praised for his faith (see Gen 15:6).

Mary's question is really a request for a sign, since the message seems to her an impossible one. Since we have seen that the Old Testament does not find anything reprehensible in the demand for a sign, it need not be thought that Mary's faith would exclude such a request.

In his answer the angel refutes Mary's objection and thus confirms the message: by God's special intervention she will become the mother of the Messiah. 'Holy Spirit' and 'power of the Most High' are parallel expressions. Compare Acts 1:8, 'But you shall receive power when the Holy Spirit has come upon you'. The verbs 'come upon' and 'overshadow' are also parallel expressions. 'Come upon' often refers to God's intervention in human affairs (see Lk 21:26; Acts 1:8; 8:24; 13:40). 'Overshadow' is used elsewhere in the gospels only of the cloud at the transfiguration (Mk 9:7; Mt 17:5; Lk 9:34). The expression recalls the cloud which covered the tent of meeting (Ex 40:34–35) and the glory of Yahweh which filled the tabernacle. The phrase expresses the presence of God's mighty power. John was to be 'filled with the Holy Spirit, even from his mother's womb' (Lk 1:15), but Jesus' conception and birth are the effect of a unique demonstration of God's power.

In Lk 1:32 the phrase 'Son of the Most High' is a title to be understood within the Jewish messianic perspective. Most probably it does not imply divinity. But here in Lk 1:35 the situation is different. 'Therefore' (*dio kai*, literally 'wherefore also') refers back to God's powerful intervention. 'The child to be born will be called holy', that is, through God's powerful intervention he will 'be' holy. The word 'holy' refers to Dan 9:24 where we are told that the messianic times will be marked by the anointing of a holy one, or a holy place. This child will also be 'Son of God'. Here 'Son of God' definitely goes beyond the Jewish messianic perspective. The Son of God will be conceived by the Spirit or power of God alone. Jesus is united with God in a way which is not possible to conceive in the Old Testament or in Judaism. He is the 'Son of God' in an absolutely new sense.

> . . . the way these ideas are combined in [Lk] 1:35 takes us out of the realm of Jewish expectation of the Messiah into the realm of early Christianity. . . . there was no Jewish expectation that the Messiah would be God's Son in the sense of having been conceived without a male parent.
>
> The real parallel for the conglomeration of ideas in 1:35 is not an OT passage but the early Christian formulations of christology.[22]

All this clearly implies a virginal conception, but it is equally clear that this is not the first concern of the text.

If Lk 1:35 is compared with the baptism and transfiguration narratives in Mark and Luke, and with Acts 1:8 and Rom 1:3–4, it appears that Luke is describing the conception of Jesus in eschatological terms: he regards the conception itself as a *parousia*, or the coming of the Lord. The text expresses the compenetration of spirit and flesh in the body of Jesus from the time of his conception.

The parallelism between Lk 1:35 and Acts 1:8 is very close:

Lk 1:35	Acts 1:8
the power	power
come upon (descend)	come upon (descend)
the Holy Spirit	the Holy Spirit
upon you (singular)	upon you (plural)

If the context is taken into account, the parallel becomes even clearer. As Lk 1:35 is the culminating point of the annunciation, so Acts 1:8 constitutes the point of the post-Easter encounter of Jesus and the Eleven. The latter scene is built on a pattern similar to that of the annunciation: encounter (Acts 1:3), first part of the message (Acts 1:4–5), question of the Eleven (Acts 1:6), second part of the message (Acts 1:7–8), departure (Acts 1:9). In an even wider context Lk 1:35

and Acts 1:8 are seen to occupy analogous positions at the beginning of each part of Luke's two-volume work: they serve as introductions to what will be the principal subject of the book which follows: Jesus in the gospel, the Church in Acts.

Similarly, almost every term in Rom 1:4 has an equivalent in Lk 1:35:

Rom 1:4	Lk 1:35
according to the Spirit of holiness	the Holy Spirit
in power	and the power
designated Son of God	will be called Son of God
(by his resurrection from the dead)	(to be born)

The parallelism of the two passages is reinforced by the context, which in Rom 1:3 as in Lk 1:27, 33 emphasizes the Davidic origin of Jesus. The most striking, however, is the convergence, in Paul and Luke, of the three fundamental themes of the Spirit, the power, and divine filiation. Luke, therefore, did not invent the relation between the Spirit, the power, and divine filiation. His originality consists in bringing together the three themes in a coherent Christological synthesis which occurs several times in Luke-Acts, and in tracing this synthesis to the origins of Jesus, unlike the earlier tradition which saw in the resurrection the investiture of Jesus as Son of God in power. Being a synthesis of Luke's theology, Lk 1:35 is clearly redactional.

The combination of Lk 1:32–33 and Lk 1:35 is an example of a superposition typical of a two-level Christology, expressed in the double title Son of David–Son of God, which is widespread in the New Testament. It has been noted that Luke has a preference for binary constructions. If Lk 1:32–35 is constructed according to that technique, it means that the faith in Christ announced by the Lucan Church (Lk 1:35) corresponds to the promises of the Old Testament (Lk 1:32–33). The Christ in whom we believe is the fulfilment of the messianic promises. Other examples of this binary construction (Lk 22:15–20; 22:66–71; 24:47–48) lead to the conclusion that the two terms of the binary construction in Luke have an identical content. The binary construction always represents the *tradition* received by Luke and the *interpretation* he gives to it. By its combination of an expression of Christological faith of the Hellenistic type with a fragment of a hymn originating in Judeo-Christianity, the construction of Lk 1:32–35 reflects the encounter of Jewish Christianity and a Christianity open to Hellenism, and thus reveals Luke's concern to translate the message for his time.

After the confirmation of the message, the angel announces the sign: 'Your kinswoman Elizabeth in her old age has also conceived a son'. This is very close to God's words to Abraham in relation to the promised birth of Isaac (Gen 18:14). The last part of the angel's reply, 'for with God nothing will be impossible', can be fully understood if Mary's question meant: This is impossible. The same idea is expressed in Gen 18:14, 'Is anything too hard for the Lord?'

> **Verse 38:** And Mary said, 'Behold, I am the handmaid of the Lord; let it be to me according to your word.' And the angel departed from her.

Mary's reply may contain an allusion to I Sam 1:11, 'If you will indeed look on the affliction of your maidservant (= handmaid), but will give to your maidservant a son, then I will give him to the Lord . . .'. It may also refer to Ps 123(122):2, 'as the eyes of a maid to the hand of her mistress, so our eyes look to the Lord our God, till he have mercy upon us'. Some have sought an historical reminiscence in the final response of Mary to the annunciation in Lk 1:38, but it should be said that the portrait of Mary in Lk 1:38 is rather shaped from Luke's account of her in Jesus' ministry (see Luke's rewriting of Mk 3:31–35 in Lk 8:19–21). By stressing Mary's acceptance of God's word, Luke associates Mary with the *anawim* or 'poor ones' who were totally dependent on God for support. Luke will develop this last point in the *Magnificat*.

The actual fulfilment of the announcement of Lk 1:35 must be supposed to follow after the departure (= the leave-taking) of the angel. But in this case we have no counterpart to Lk 1:24 announcing that after these days Elizabeth conceived.

On the basis of the annunciation narrative as it stands, we cannot claim that at this point Mary knew all that her role in the redemption would entail. But she did freely and consciously agree to the conception of a son, who would be son of God and Messiah. By her *fiat* Mary expressed consent to the fulfilment of God's salvific work in Jesus. But this does not mean that Mary was fully enlightened about whatever this would imply (see Lk 2:19, 50, 51). Her *fiat* was essentially an act of faith (Lk 1:45), and for Mary too faith is as much darkness as light. Mary is first of all a figure of faith, and even the primordial figure and archetype of the faith of the disciple. This viewpoint is not confined to the infancy narrative; it is also found in Lk 11:27–28 and Acts 1:14.

To the best of her knowledge Mary committed herself to God, but she had to learn gradually that God's thoughts and ways are not those of men. And at more than one point in her life she did not understand (Lk 2:50). Like Jesus' disciples, Mary came to understand the mystery of her Son only after and in the light of Easter.

The visitation and Magnificat (Lk 1:39–56)

This is a complementary episode to the annunciation of the birth of Jesus, which has no counterpart in the narrative about John the Baptist. The visitation is first of all an answer to the sign given by the angel

The annunciations to Mary and to the shepherds have, in this respect, an identical construction. After having received from the angel the 'sign' of the child in the manger (Lk 2:12), the shepherds 'went with haste' (*speusantes*) to see what had happened (Lk 2:16). Likewise, Mary, informed about the sign of Elizabeth's pregnancy, 'went with haste' (*meta spoudēs*) to see her cousin. By doing so, she assures the encounter of the prophet and the Lord (Lk 1:42–45). Indeed, the focal point of the account is the encounter of Jesus and John the Baptist rather than that of their mothers.

Verses 39–41: In those days Mary arose and went with haste into the hill country, to a city of Judah, (40) and she entered the house of Zechariah and greeted Elizabeth. (41) And when Elizabeth heard the greeting of Mary, the babe leaped in her womb; and Elizabeth was filled with the Holy Spirit

Immediately after the departure of the angel, 'Mary went with haste' to visit Elizabeth and to establish the sign. A sign is not to be taken for granted, and Mary hastens to see her relative. Her 'haste' is an expression of her obedience to the plan revealed to her by the angel. Compare this with Lk 2:15–16: 'When the angels went away from them. . . . "Let us go over to Bethlehem and see this thing that has happened, which the Lord has made known to us." And they went with haste. . . .'

In *response* to Mary's greeting, the baby in Elizabeth's womb moves. The movement of the child is probably to be understood as the occasion of Elizabeth's inspiration. We were told in Lk 1:15 that John 'will be filled with the Holy Spirit, even from his mother's womb', and thus would be a prophet (see also Lk 1:17), and John begins to prophesy by jumping with gladness in his mother's womb. Elizabeth is able to discern a special significance in an incident which she would have considered perfectly natural in other circumstances. Elizabeth is now 'filled with the Holy Spirit', and she speaks as a prophetess.

Verses 42–45: and she exclaimed with a loud cry, 'Blessed are you among women, and blessed is the fruit of your womb! (43) And why is this granted me, that the mother of my Lord should come to me? (44) For behold, when the voice of your greeting came to my ears, the babe in my womb leaped for joy. (45) And blessed is she who believed that there would be a fulfilment of what was spoken to her from the Lord.'

Elizabeth's words 'blessed are you among women' have a comparative, not an absolutely superlative, value both in Greek and in Hebrew. They mean that Mary has been specially blessed by God, but not necessarily that she is the most blessed of all women, for the same can be said of other women. Indeed, Elizabeth's words are reminiscent of Judg 5:24, 'most blessed of women be Jael', and Judith 13:18, 'O daughter, you are blessed by the Most High above all women on earth'. 'Blessed is the fruit of your womb' echoes Deut 28:1, 4, the blessing promised by Moses to Israel if Israel was obedient to the voice of God: '. . . blessed shall be the fruit of your body'. If we take Lk 1:42 and 45, 'blessed is she who believed', together, we notice also a striking parallel with Lk 11:27–28, 'Blessed is the womb that bore you. . . . Blessed rather are those who hear the word of God and keep it.' Elizabeth's expression of unworthiness, 'why is this granted me, that the mother of my Lord should come to me?', echoes that of David in the presence of the Ark of Yahweh, 'How can the ark of the Lord come to me?' (II Sam 6:9).

Then follows the *Magnificat*. Like the *Benedictus* and the *Nunc Dimittis*, it has received its name from the first words of the Vulgate Latin version. There is no need to discuss here whether the *Magnificat* was originally attributed to Mary, as favoured by most Greek manuscripts, or to Elizabeth, as favoured by some Latin versions which are possibly closer to the original text. In any case, it is a literary mosaic of Old Testament texts which should not as such be attributed to Mary, or Elizabeth. The *Magnificat* is written in the form of a thanksgiving psalm. It is a chain of Old Testament references and, it seems, derives especially from the canticle of Hannah (I Sam 2:1–10). The *Magnificat* resembles ancient Jewish hymns which were sung by the people thanking God who saved them in spite of their weakness. The early Church celebrated God's marvellous interventions in similar hymns. It is possible that Luke wished to express the belief that the events of Lk 1 – 2 were the culminating instance of God's filling the poor with riches and faithfully fulfilling his promises.

It is highly improbable, then, that the *Magnificat* represents the authentic words of Mary. We would rather consider it Luke's editing of an early Christian hymn. It has been noted that there is no explicit reference to the birth of the Messiah, which is rather surprising after the annunciation and Elizabeth's welcome. It is possible, therefore, that the *Magnificat* is a Lucan adaptation of a Jewish hymn, more specifically a thanksgiving hymn from the circle of the *anawim* or poor of Yahweh who assumed an important role in the religious life of Israel after the Babylonian exile, or from a similar Jewish Christian group. While the 'poor' referred to in the Old Testament are usually economically poor, the term *anawim* expresses not so much an economic status as an attitude of complete readiness for and dependence on God, two characteristics of true humility before God (see Zeph 2:3; 3:11f.) Ideas expressed in these circles could easily serve the purpose of a writer who wanted to express the feelings of one who called herself the handmaid of the Lord.

Whatever its exact origin, the *Magnificat* has at least been edited and placed within its present framework by Luke to convey certain theological ideas. If in any way Luke is responsible for the hymn, he definitely shows his familiarity with the spirituality of the *anawim* circles to which Mary presumably belonged. However, the *Magnificat* does not permit us to describe the actual feelings of Mary, but rather to know what the evangelist – and the early Church – had to tell us about her.

Many suggestions have been made concerning the division of the *Magnificat* into two, three, or four parts. We present here a division into four parts:

(1)   Joyful thankfulness for personal blessing (vv. 46–48);
(2)   God's mercy for all who fear him (vv. 49–50);
(3)   God's intervention for those of low degree (vv. 51–53);
(4)   God's special love for his people Israel (vv. 54–55).

The divine benefits mentioned in Lk 1:51–53 illustrate the affirmation in Lk 1:50 of God's mercy towards those who fear him. The second half of the *Magnificat* describes God's victorious intervention in terms of a national liberation from any kind of oppression. This is a recurrent aspect of Old Testament messianism. The New Testament rethinks this and transfers the idea of total victory to the Messiah's parousia.

> The poverty and hunger of the oppressed in the Magnificat are primarily spiritual, but we should not forget the physical realities faced by the early Christians. The first followers of Jesus were Galileans; and Galilee, victimized by the absentee ownership of estates (cf. Luke 20:9), was a spawning ground of first-century revolts against a repressive occupation and the taxation it engendered (Acts 5:37; ...). There was real poverty among the Jerusalem Christians who became the nucleus of the post-resurrection Church. ... And Luke's peculiar and emphatic castigation of wealth (6:24–26; 12:19–20; 16:25; 21:1–4) points to the existence of many poor in the communities to be served by Luke's Gospel. And so vss. 51–53 of the Magnificat would resonate among such groups; for them the Christian good news meant that the ultimately blessed were not the mighty and the rich who tyrannized them.[23]

Verses 46–48: And Mary said, 'My soul magnifies the Lord, (47) and my spirit rejoices in God my Saviour, (48) for he has regarded the low estate of his handmaiden. For behold, henceforth all generations will call me blessed;

Although the broad sequence of ideas is closer to the canticle of Hannah (I Sam 2:1–10) than to any other Old Testament text, yet the verbal parallels are not marked, and the opening verses, Lk 1:46–47, are strikingly different.

'My soul magnifies the Lord.' The term 'soul' here should not be understood as we do in the expression 'body and soul'. In most instances where the Bible uses the word 'soul', we should understand 'self' or 'I'. The Hebrew word *nephesh* underlying 'soul' means the totality of a person. The Hebrew word for 'spirit', *ruah*, indicates the life principle. When a person dies, it is not his soul, in the Greek sense of the word, but his *breath of life* or *spirit* that leaves him. For all practical purposes we may translate both 'soul' and 'spirit' as 'I'. Written in typical psalm style and parallelism, verses 46–47 contain several phrases which remind us of I Sam 2:1, 'My heart exults in the Lord; my strength is exalted in the Lord. My mouth derides my enemies, because I rejoice in your salvation.' The rest of the opening words (v. 47) is close to the words of Hab 3:18, 'Yet I will rejoice in the Lord, I will joy in the God of my salvation'.

Verse 48 seems to reproduce Hannah's words, 'if you will indeed look on the affliction of your maidservant, and remember me, and not forget your maidservant . . .' (I Sam 1:11). The term 'low estate' (*tapeinōsis*) is often descriptive of the persecution or oppression from which God delivers his people (Deut 26:7; Ps 136[135]:23). Upon closer inspection it appears that the connection between Lk 1:48 and I Sam 1:11 is not exclusive and that one should also take into account echoes from Gen 29:32; 30:13, both referring to Leah after childbirth.

Ps 34(33), an individual psalm of thanksgiving, shows how various phrases and ideas of the *Magnificat* are already found together in the Old Testament. It includes phrases like 'my soul', the salvation of the 'poor', 'those who fear the Lord', who shall lack no 'good thing', and it affirms that God saves the 'crushed in spirit'.

Although every word in verses 46–47 can be traced to a psalm passage, one feature is not found in the Book of Psalms, viz. the exact equivalence of 'soul' (Hebrew *nephesh* or Greek *psuchē*) and 'spirit' (Hebrew *ruah* or Greek *pneuma*), expressed in parallelism. However, this feature is found in Isa 26:9, 'My soul yearns for you in the night, my spirit within me earnestly seeks you'. Similarly, Job 12:10, 'In his hand is the life (*nephesh, psuchē*) of every living thing, and the breath (*ruah, pneuma*) of all mankind'. And Wisdom 15:11, 'because he failed to know the one who formed him, and inspired him with an active soul and breathed into him a living spirit'. Summing up, one may say that while verses 46–47 look like a straight quotation, in reality they are not.

Verses 49–50: 'for he who is mighty has done great things to me, and holy is his name. (50) And his mercy is on those who fear him from generation to generation.'

Ps 111(110):2, 9, 'Great are the works of the Lord, studied by all who have pleasure in them. . . . He sent redemption to his people; he has commanded his covenant forever. Holy and terrible is his name', may have inspired much of the wording of Lk 1:49. But in the first line of the verse we discover also a close parallel with Deut 10:21, 'He is your praise; he is your God, who has done for you these great and terrible things which your eyes have seen'. Verse 49 says that the blessing of the handmaid is part of the great salvation event.

Verse 50 is very close to Ps 103(102):17, 'But the steadfast love of the Lord is from everlasting to everlasting upon those who fear him'. It parallels and amplifies the thought of v. 49. God's 'mercy' refers back to the 'great things' mentioned in Lk 1:49. The thought that God has done great things occurs frequently in Deuteronomy, the Psalms and the prophets. But here in the *Magnificat* these 'great things' are specified in vv. 51–53 which describe God's special love for the lowly, and especially in vv. 54–55 which show that the event is the realization of the promises 'to Abraham and to his posterity', and therefore the salvation-event *par excellence*.

Verses 51–53: 'He has shown strength with his arm, he has scattered the proud in the imagination of their hearts, (52) he has put down the mighty from their thrones, and exalted those of low degree; (53) he has filled the hungry with good things, and the rich he has sent empty away.'

These verses continue the description of God's saving intervention in phrases and concepts familiar to those who were 'looking for the consolation of Israel' (Lk 2:25) and 'for the redemption of Jerusalem' (Lk 2:38). Verse 51 recalls Ps 89(88): 10, 'You did crush Rahab like a carcass, you did scatter your enemies with your arm'. [24] The verse says that God displays his power and brings to nothing the plans of those who are arrogant.

Verse 52 makes clear that the primary thought of these verses is that of vindication of Israel by the defeat of its enemies. It is also the chief basis of comparison with the canticle of Hannah, especially I Sam 2:7, 'The Lord makes poor and makes rich; he brings low, he also exalts'. But a closer look at the two passages shows that there is no exact equivalence and that, on the whole, Sir 10:14 is verbally closer: 'The Lord has cast down the thrones of rulers, and has seated the lowly in their place'.

Verse 53 develops the same contrast. The underlying text this time is apparently I Sam 2:5, 'Those who were full have hired themselves out for bread, but those who were hungry have ceased to hunger'. However, the language is derived from several sources including Ps 107(106):9, 'For he satisfies him who is thirsty, and the hungry he fills with good things', and Ps 146(145):7, 'who executes justice for the oppressed, who gives food to the hungry'. There may also be echoes in Ps 103(102):5, 'who satisfies you with good as long as you live', and Ps 34(33):10, 'The young lions suffer want and hunger; but those who seek the Lord lack no good thing'. Some have compared the contrast between the hungry and the rich with the story of the Rich Man and Lazarus, found only in Lk 16:19–31.

It has been said that the *Magnificat* is one of the most revolutionary documents in all literature, containing three separate revolutions:

(1) 'He has shown strength with his arm, he has scattered the proud in the imagination of their hearts' (Lk 1:51). This is a *moral* revolution.
(2) 'He has put down the mighty from their thrones, and exalted those of low degree' (Lk 1:52). This is a *social* revolution.
(3) 'He has filled the hungry with good things, and the rich he has sent empty away' (Lk 1:53). This is an *economic* revolution.

Taken together, vv. 51–53 give expression to the reversal which will take place in the New Age.

Verses 54–55: 'He has helped his servant Israel, in remembrance of his mercy, (55) as he spoke to our fathers, to Abraham and to his posterity for ever.'

God's saving intervention is now described in terms that are found frequently in the Old Testament. The closest parallels are Isa 41:8, 'But you, Israel, my servant, Jacob, whom I have chosen, the offspring of Abraham, my friend'; and Ps 98(97):3, 'He has remembered his steadfast love and faithfulness to the house of Israel'. The phrase 'his steadfast love and faithfulness' reminds us of God's covenant with his people.

The language of v. 55 is very similar to Mic 7:20, 'You will show faithfulness to Jacob and steadfast love to Abraham, as you have sworn to our fathers from the days of old'. See also Gen 17:7, 'And I will establish my covenant between me and you and your descendants after you throughout their generations for an everlasting covenant, to be God to you and to your descendants after you'.

In the *Magnificat* Luke reflects on the history of Israel. He interprets the 'great things' which God has done as the fulfilment of the promises to the fathers which had hitherto remained unfulfilled. This means that the saving intervention of God, recalled in this canticle, was so important that it could be considered as the climax of all previous divine interventions and therefore of the Old Testament as a whole. One may rightly wonder whether a Jew would speak and write like this.

It seems that only a Christian would combine the Old Testament expressions into such an impressive and decisive statement.

But it remains strange, especially after the welcoming words of Elizabeth, that God's saving intervention is not pictured in more concrete terms, that it does not contain any explicit reference to the birth of the Messiah. It has been suggested that this is because Luke has thoroughly edited an older hymn. Recently, it has even been suggested that the canticles of Luke's infancy narrative were originally spoken in Aramaic, then recorded in Hebrew and handed on to us in Greek translation made in an early Christian community. Luke, then, improved on their style when he included them in his work. At all events, the *Magnificat*, like the whole of the infancy narrative, forms a bridge between the Old and the New Testament, and this appears in its form as well as in its language.

> **Verse 56:** And Mary remained with her about three months, and returned to her home.

The fact that Mary's departure is mentioned before the description of John's birth does not necessarily mean that she departed before the child was born. If we take all this literally, it would seem that Mary, who visited Elizabeth in her sixth month and then stayed for about three months, left her kinswoman a few days before the birth! We are dealing here, however, with one of Luke's literary devices. Before passing on to the next episode, Luke rounds off the present one. The *leave-taking* is one of the typical *seams* of Luke's narrative.

The fact that Mary returns to her *own* home seems to imply that Joseph had not yet brought her to his home. But, strictly speaking, there is nothing that allows us to determine whether Luke thinks of 'her home' as the home of her parents or the home of Joseph. Luke states that at the time of Jesus' birth Mary was living with Joseph, but he passes over the details of their coming together.

Summary

In the first section of his infancy narrative Luke affirms the following:

(1)   The messianic times are inaugurated with the annunciation of the births of John and Jesus. These are narrated in a parallel manner, but John is clearly subordinate to Jesus.
(2)   The messianic times are not to be characterized by spectacular apocalyptic events, but the people are to prepare themselves for the fulfilment of God's will. Faith is the criterion of this preparedness, expressed in Mary's *fiat* which prefigures the obedience of the disciple.
(3)   The messianic times are times of reversal and revolution, though not directly in a political sense. The realization of Israel's hope

depends on whether Israel is capable of recognizing the true meaning of God's intervention, that is, of a new understanding of salvation and redemption, independent of the national interests of Israel.

(4)   These new developments are in continuity with God's promises to Abraham and the Fathers, but through the agency of the Holy Spirit they surpass whatever these men of old may have expected.

7　The Birth Narratives

(Exegesis of Lk 1:57 – 2:52)

The birth and manifestation of John (Lk 1:57–80)

This section of the infancy narrative has two major divisions: the narrative (Lk 1:57–66) and the *Benedictus* (Lk 1:67–79) for which the narrative provides the setting. The conclusion of the section (Lk 1:80) connects these events with the further story of John the Baptist (see Lk 3:1–20).

> **Verses 57–58:** Now the time came for Elizabeth to be delivered, and she gave birth to a son.
>
> (58) And her neighbours and kinsfolk heard that the Lord had shown great mercy to her, and they rejoiced with her.

Like Lk 1:7, verses 57–58 refer to the situation of the barren wives of the patriarchs to whom God gave joy through the gift of a child. While verse 57 seems to echo Gen 25:24, Rebekah's giving birth to Esau and Jacob, verse 58 refers to Sarah's words in Gen 21:6.

The birth of John the Baptist marks the fulfilment of Gabriel's message to Zechariah. Verse 57 says literally, 'Now to Elizabeth was fulfilled the time to bear her son', and suggests the fulfilment of the messianic times. Compare Lk 2:6 which says literally, 'there was fulfilled to her the day to bear a son'. The idea of fulfilment or completion is also found in Lk 2:21–22 which says literally, 'And when were completed eight days. . . . And were completed the days of cleansing. . . .'

'And her neighbours and kinsfolk . . . rejoiced with her': this is a fulfilment of the promise found in Lk 1:14, 'And you will have joy and gladness, and many will rejoice at his birth'. Joy is a key-word of the infancy narrative (see Lk 1:14, 58; 2:10; the root of the word found in these passages is the same as that found in Lk 1:28, 'Hail', or better, 'Rejoice').

> **Verses 59–61:** And on the eighth day they came to circumcise the child; and they would have named him Zechariah after his father.

(60) but his mother said, 'Not so; he shall be called John.'

(61) And they said to her, 'None of your kindred is called by this name.'

The ceremony of circumcision took place on the eighth day after the birth, according to the prescriptions of Gen 17:12 and Lev 12:3. It had become customary to name the child on that day, and it is apparently because of the name-giving that Luke narrates this incident. In opposition to the relatives' intention to call him Zechariah, Elizabeth insists that he is to be called John.

Verses 62–66: And they made signs to his father, inquiring what he would have him called.

(63) And he asked for a writing tablet, and wrote, 'His name is John.' And they all marvelled.

(64) And immediately his mouth was opened and his tongue loosed, and he spoke, blessing God.

(65) And fear came on all their neighbours. And all these things were talked about through all the hill country of Judea;

(66) and all who heard them laid them up in their hearts, saying, 'What then will this child be?' For the hand of the Lord was with him.

Throughout the Bible a name is more than a label. It is closely related to the character and nature of the bearer, whether he is God or a man. For instance, we read in Ps 9:10, 'And those who know your name put their trust in you'. This certainly does not mean that those who know God is called Yahweh will put their trust in him. It means rather that those who know what God is like will be ready to trust him in everything. People like Abram and Simon have their names changed by God to indicate that they become altogether different persons. Pious people like Zechariah and Elizabeth choose a name expressive of their own faith and gratitude, or of their hopes for the child. John stands for *Jehohanan* or *Johanan* which means 'God's gracious gift'. The name may here express the grateful acknowledgement of God's unexpected mercy and goodness in the gift of a son to ageing parents.

Zechariah 'asked for a writing tablet', a small wooden board covered with wax, 'and wrote, "His name is John" '. These words refer to the pronouncement at Lk 1:13, 'you shall call his name John'. The name has been determined by God himself.

'And they all marvelled.' The relatives and neighbours sense that there is more behind this name. The preceding events indicate that both Zechariah and Elizabeth are acting under divine guidance.

'And immediately his mouth was opened.' The angel had said that Zechariah would be 'silent and unable to speak until the day that these things come to pass' (Lk 1:20). The moment has arrived and

Zechariah's dumbness is removed. We may have here an additional argument for our opinion that Zechariah's dumbness was originally understood as a sign. Now that everything has happened as announced by the angel there is no longer any need for a sign, and so Zechariah's dumbness is removed and he praises God. The content of that praise is given in the *Benedictus*.

The evangelist first records the reaction of those present: 'And fear came on all their neighbours': not the fear men feel in the presence of danger but the religious awe of people who experience a divine miracle. This feature may be related to the apocalyptic atmosphere of the narrative: 'all who heard them laid them up in their hearts' (Lk 1:66; see Dan 7:28, and also Lk 2:19, 51).

Luke rounds off the narrative part of this section with the expectant question, 'What then will this child be?' and ends with a biblical expression peculiar to Luke in the New Testament: 'the hand of the Lord was with him' (see Jer 26:24; Acts 11:21; 13:11), i.e. he enjoyed God's protection and would be a mighty instrument of God.

The *Benedictus*, like the *Magnificat*, is a chain of Old Testament quotations and allusions and may well have been a pre-existing psalm which Luke has worked over and attributed to Zechariah.

The literary structure of the canticle is centred on the parallelism of the 'covenant' and the 'oath' in verses 72–73, which is based on such texts as Gen 17:4 and 22:16–17, Ps 89(88):4, 35–37 and Ps 105(104):8–9. The rest of the canticle forms a pattern of concentric symmetry around these two central verses with key-words repeated or paralleled in inverse order in each half of the canticle.

To illustrate this clearly we give the text of the canticle, indicating the corresponding elements by A-A, B-B, etc. starting from the central verses 72–73. The first and the last words of the canticle are in small capitals because, in the mind of the Israelites, these were very closely related. They are indeed two forms of greeting, one applied to God, 'blessed', the other to men, 'peace'.

F 1:68 BLESSED be the Lord *God* of Israel, for he has *visited*
E and redeemed *his people*,

1:69 and has raised up a horn of *salvation* for us in the house of his servant David,

1:70 as he spoke
D by the mouth of his holy *prophets* from of old,

C 1:71 that we should be *saved* from *our enemies*, and *from the hand* of all who hate us;

B 1:72 to perform the mercy promised to *our fathers*,
A and to remember his holy COVENANT,

A   1:73   the OATH which he swore
B   to *our father* Abraham,

        1:74   to grant us
C   that we, being *delivered from the hand* of *our enemies*, might serve him without fear,

        1:75   in holiness and righteousness before him all the days of our life.

        1:76   And you, child,
D   will be called the *prophet* of the Most High; and you will go before the Lord to prepare his ways,

E   1:77   to give knowledge of *salvation* to *his people* in the forgiveness of their sins,

F   1:78   through the tender mercy of our *God* when the day shall *visit* (RSV: dawn upon) us from on high

        1:79   to give light to those who sit in darkness and in the shadow of death, to guide our feet into the way of PEACE.

Each half of the canticle contains a similar structure. Thus the whole is built around three dominant themes:

(1)   God's benevolent intervention;
(2)   the salvation of the people;
(3)   the word of God.

Indicating these themes by their respective numbers, we get the following picture of the canticle: 1-2-3-2-1-3 // 3-1-2-3-2-1.

	Blessed be God for his	1:68a
(1)	BENEVOLENT INTERVENTION, which leads to the	1:68b
(2)	SALVATION OF THE PEOPLE, in accordance with the	1:69
(3)	PROPHETIC WORD, which announced the	1:70
(2)	SALVATION OF THE PEOPLE, through the	1:71
(1)	BENEVOLENT INTERVENTION, according to the	1:72a
(3)	WORD OF THE COVENANT	1:72b
(3)	the WORD OF THE OATH, assuring the	1:73a
(1)	BENEVOLENT INTERVENTION for the	1:73b
(2)	SALVATION OF THE PEOPLE	1:74–75
(3)	The WORD OF GOD DESIGNATING the prophet prepares the	1:76
(2)	SALVATION OF THE PEOPLE through the	1:77
(1)	BENEVOLENT INTERVENTION of God in a Messiah who leads us to peace.	1:78 / 1:79

The first section of the canticle (Lk 1:68–72), in successive parallelisms, extols God for his messianic deliverance and rejoices in its results. Since the *Benedictus* celebrates the redemption which God accomplished through Jesus, the Davidic Messiah, it is significant that its initial words, 'Blessed be the Lord God of Israel', echo the words spoken by David when his son Solomon acceded to the throne, thereby assuring the Davidic line of succession (I Kgs 1:48). Expressing absolute certainty concerning its fulfilment, Zechariah speaks of the coming redemption as an accomplished fact: God 'has visited his people'. In the Old Testament God visits his people either to liberate them or to punish them. Here the visitation and redemption refer to the sending of the Messiah, the 'horn of salvation' of the house of David. Compare Ps 111(110):9, 'He sent redemption to his people, he has commanded his covenant forever', and Ps 132(131):17, 'There I will make a horn to sprout for David'. The 'horn' is the emblem of strength. Compare Ps 18(17):2, 'The Lord is . . . my shield, and the horn of my salvation, my stronghold'. According to God's purpose, expressed by the holy prophets, the Messiah will be sent to save his people from their enemies. This will be the ultimate fulfilment of God's kindness and mercy in remembrance of his holy covenant and of the oath sworn to Abraham. Lk 1:70–72 suggests Ps 106(105):10, 45, 'So he saved them from the hand of the foe, and delivered them from the power of the enemy. . . . He remembered for their sake his covenant. . . .'

The second section (Lk 1:73–79) describes the place which John occupies in this mighty act of God. Lk 1:73–75 recalls Ps 105(104):8–9, 42, 'He is mindful of his covenant forever . . . the covenant which he made with Abraham, his sworn promise to Isaac. . . . For he remembered his holy promise, and Abraham his servant.' The switch from the third person to the second (Lk 1:76) is a literary device by which the force of the poem is intensified. Verse 76 refers to Isa 40:3, 'In the wilderness prepare the way of the Lord, make straight in the desert a highway for our God'. It echoes Lk 3:4, 'The voice of one crying in the wilderness: Prepare the way of the Lord', as well as Lk 7:27, 'Behold I send my messenger before your face, who shall prepare your way before you'. Verse 79 recalls Ps 107(106):10, 'Some sat in darkness and in gloom, prisoners in affliction and in irons', Isa 9:2(9:1 in Hebrew), 'The people who walked in darkness have seen a great light', and Isa 42:7, 'to bring out the prisoners from the dungeon, from the prison those who sit in darkness'. Verses 76 and 79, addressed to John, point to his vocation of prophet and forerunner.

'Salvation through the forgiveness of sins' is a typically Lucan formula which, with minor differences, is found ten times in Luke-Acts, and only once in Mark and Matthew (see e.g., Lk 3:8; 5:32; Acts 3:19, 26; 5:31). Salvation is the result of God's loving kindness and mercy and will be realized 'when the day (*anatolē*) shall dawn upon us from on high'. In line with Mal 4:2(3:20 in Hebrew) and to some extent Isa 60:1, *anatolē* suggests the image of the 'rising sun', that is, the Messiah or the messianic age. This rising sun will 'give light to those who sit in darkness', that is, the darkness of sin, and will 'guide our feet into the way of peace', that is, will guide men to justice without which there cannot be true peace.

> **Verse 80:** And the child grew and became strong in spirit, and he was in the wilderness till the day of his manifestation to Israel.

Luke concludes the infancy story of John the Baptist by one of his literary *seams*, a *refrain of growth* (see Lk 2:40, 52), indicating John's physical and spiritual growth in words reminiscent of Samson, 'and the boy grew, and the Lord blessed him. And the spirit of the Lord began to stir him' (Judg 13:24f.) and Samuel, 'Now the boy Samuel continued to grow both in stature and in favour with the Lord and with men '(I Sam 2:26; compare Lk 2:52).

The reference to John's stay in the wilderness of Judah prepares the way for Lk 3:2, 'the word of God came to John the son of Zechariah in the wilderness'. In the light of the discoveries at Qumran, situated in the wilderness of Judah, it is interesting to speculate whether John's stay in the wilderness may not have been spent in one of the ascetic communities in the neighbourhood of the Dead Sea. The present state of studies, however, does not allow us to give a decisive answer to this question.

The birth of Jesus (Lk 2:1–20)

The description of the circumstances of time and place (Lk 2:1–5) and the birth of Jesus (Lk 2:6–7) are, as it were, a prologue to the story of the shepherds (Lk 2:8–20). Indeed, the narrative focuses not on Jesus' birth but on the angelic interpretation of that birth for the shepherds, and their reaction to the good news. Lk 2:8–20 is a self-contained section or inclusion, framed by verse 8, 'there were shepherds out in the field', and verse 20, 'and the shepherds returned'. But within this self-contained unit one can distinguish the apocalyptic vision in which an annunciation is made (Lk 2:8–14) and the reaction (Lk 2:15–20), first of the shepherds (Lk 2:15–17), and then of the hearers and Mary (Lk 2:18–20). The shepherds' 'praising God' (Lk 2:20) repeats the terminology of Lk 2:13, 'a multitude of the heavenly host praising God'. The clause 'all they had heard and seen' (Lk 2:20) is a recapitulatory summary of the vision (Lk 2:9–14) and the finding of the child (Lk 2:15–17), where it was exactly 'as it had been told them' (Lk 2:20) in verse 12.

The narrative of the shepherds is the natural continuation of the birth of the child at Bethlehem (Lk 2:1–7), but certainly constitutes a clearly delineated section which must be studied as such. The apocalyptic vision is its central part. Some feel that the climax of Lk 2:1–20 comes in Lk 2:15–20, where the protagonists of Lk 2:1–7, Mary, Joseph, and the baby, and of Lk 2:8–14, shepherds, join each other. But it is in Lk 2:8–14 that 'heaven and earth touch' in and through the angels who interpret the meaning of the birth that has taken place at Bethlehem.

It has been suggested that a midrashic reflection on Gen 35:21 and Mic 4:8, both referring to Migdal Eder, 'Tower of the Flock', close to a mention of Bethlehem (Gen 35:19; Mic 5:2[1]), underlies Lk 2:8–20. In fact, several motifs found in Mic 4 – 5 have parallels in Lk 2:1–20: for instance, the flow of peoples and nations to Jerusalem (compare the movement of 'the whole world' caused by the census of Augustus), and the 'woman in birthpangs'.

Verses 1–5: In those days a decree went out from Caesar Augustus that all the world should be enrolled. (2) This was the first enrolment, when Quirinius was governor of Syria. (3) And all went to be enrolled, each to his own city. (4) And Joseph also went up from Galilee, from the city of Nazareth, to Judea, to the city of David, which is called Bethlehem, because he was of the house and lineage of David, (5) to be enrolled with Mary, his betrothed, who was with child.

Augustus was emperor from 30 B.C. to A.D. 14.

The name of Augustus would evoke memories and ideals for Luke's readers. In 29 B.C., one hundred years before Luke wrote this Gospel, Augustus had brought an end to almost a century of civil war that had ravaged the Roman realms; and at last the doors of the shrine of Janus in the Forum, thrown open in times of war, were able to be closed. The Age of Augustus was propagandized as the glorious age of pastoral rule over a world made peaceful by virtue. . . . He was hailed at Halicarnassus as the 'saviour of the whole world'; and the Priene inscription grandiosely proclaimed: 'the birthday of the god marked the beginning of the good news for the world.' Luke contradicts this propaganda by showing that paradoxically the edict of Augustus served to provide the setting for the birth of Jesus. Men built an altar to the *pax Augustae*, but a heavenly chorus proclaimed the *pax Christi*: 'On earth peace to those favored by God' (2:14). The birthday that marked the true beginning of a new time took place not in Rome but in Bethlehem, and a counterclaim to man-made inscriptions was the heraldic cry of the angel of the Lord: 'I announce to you the good news of a great joy which will be for the whole people: To you this day there is born in the city of David a Savior who is Messiah and Lord' (2:10–11).[25]

The general census of 'all the world', that is, of the Roman empire (literally, *oikoumēnē*, the inhabited world), was a means of tax assessment. It is called 'first' because no Roman census had been held in Judea before that of Quirinius in A.D. 6–7, which Luke may have wrongly fixed at the time of Herod through association with Lk 1:5. The chronological difficulties raised by Lk 2:2 are still unsolved. The available evidence is insufficient for any firm solution. Luke's chief interest is to describe the birth of Jesus against the background of the Roman empire and to explain how Jesus happened to be born in Bethlehem. He understands these historical circumstances as a providential way of assuring that Jesus would be born in Bethlehem. Because of the circumstances mentioned, Joseph, who 'was of the house and lineage of David', went from Nazareth to the birthplace of his ancestor, namely Bethlehem.

> Luke's mention of the census would also have a meaning for readers who knew Jewish history. Past censuses had been causes of catastrophe. King David ordered a census for Israel and Judah (2 Sm 24) and incurred the wrath of God in the form of a pestilence. Most recently the census of Quirinius in Judea in A.D. 6–7 had provoked the rebellion of Judas the Galilean which was the beginning of the Zealot movement. It was this ultranationalistic movement which culminated in the Jewish revolt against Rome and the disastrous destruction of Jerusalem in A.D. 70. . . . Instead of being a disaster for Roman–Jewish relations, the census of Quirinius, if one understood it correctly, provided the setting for the birth of a peaceful Savior who would be a revelation to the Gentiles and a glory for the people of Israel ([Lk] 2:32). Indeed, this was the census foretold in Psalm 87:6 where God says: 'In the census of the peoples, this one will be born there'.[26]

Luke writes that Joseph '*went up* from Galilee . . . to the city of David, which is called Bethlehem'. 'To go up' is traditionally used for the journey to Jerusalem, designated as 'city of David'. Did Luke shift Micah's reference to 'the mountain of the house of the Lord' from Jerusalem to Bethlehem, since it was there that one must now go to see the Lord, for 'to you is born in the city of David a Saviour, who is Christ the Lord' (Lk 2:11)?

> **Verses 6–7:** And while they were there, the time came for her to be delivered. (7) And she gave birth to her first-born son and wrapped him in swaddling cloths, and laid him in a manger, because there was no place for them in the inn.

While they were in Bethlehem Mary gave birth to her son, her 'first-born'. The term 'first-born son' echoes the law prescribing the conse-cration of the first-born male to God (Ex 13:12; 34:19; see Lk 2:23). The first-born also received the birthright (see Gen 25:29–33). Even an only son is first-born in this sense, as can be seen from the epitaph of a Jewish woman found in Egypt and dated to 5 B.C. which reads: 'In the pains of giving birth to a first-born child, Fate brought me to the end of my life'. If she died giving birth to her first-born, clearly she had no more children. In the case of Jesus the phrase 'first-born' emphas-izes that this son has the right of inheritance to the throne of David, and does not constitute a proof that Jesus had brothers and sisters.

Mary 'wrapped him in swaddling cloths, and laid him in a manger, because there was no place for them in the inn'. There may be some value in stressing the shepherd-motif in conjunction with the Messiah's birth in the city of David, but there are no textual grounds for saying that the child, like David, is in the state of a shepherd's child because he is laid in a manger.

The 'manger' appears three times. The first time (Lk 2:7), it is the place in which the child was laid because there was no place in the inn. To allege *crowding* or *Mary's need for privacy*, as some scholars do to explain this phrase, seems to be beside the point. The note of *rejection*, which others see in the same phrase, is hardly substantiated by the statements or mood of the narration in Lk 2:1–20, or in what precedes. Notions of a cruel or inhospitable innkeeper are products of later legendary development. Like most such imaginary additions, they are out of harmony with the integrity and general atmosphere of the infancy narrative, which does not succumb to sentimentality, but is characterized by its simplicity.

One may readily surmise that the point of the narrative here concerns *the place where the child was to be*, rather than the place which suited Mary and Joseph. However, since the manger is mentioned three times (Lk 2:7, 12, 16) in apparently related instances, we will postpone the full discussion of it, as well as of the swaddling cloths and the inn, until Lk 2:16.

Verse 8: And in that region there were shepherds out in the field, keeping watch over their flock by night.

In the *Magnificat* Luke described the revolutionary character of the messianic times (Lk 1:51–53). He now illustrates how this is realized. He introduces the shepherds, a not very recommendable group of people, who are the first to receive the announcement of Jesus' birth.

Verses 9–11: And an angel of the Lord appeared to them, and the glory of the Lord shone around them, and they were filled with fear. (10) And the angel said to them, 'Be not afraid; for

behold, I bring you good news of a great joy which will come
to all the people; (11) for to you is born this day in the city of
David a Saviour, who is Christ the Lord.'

An angel of the Lord appeared to them, and the 'glory of the Lord', an
expression marking the presence of the Lord, 'shone around them'.
Just as Zechariah and Mary were troubled (Lk 1:12, 29), and Daniel
was frightened (Dan 8:17), so the shepherds were 'filled with fear', or
religious awe. Like Zechariah and Mary (Lk 1:13, 30) and Daniel
(Dan 10:12), the shepherds too are told: 'Be not afraid'. The angel's
message is an announcement of 'good news' and 'joy' to 'all the people'
of Israel. Despite the setting of Jesus' birth in the context of the Roman
empire (Lk 2:1), which was thought of as including all the inhabited
world (*oikoumēnē*), the universal aspect of salvation through Christ is
not mentioned again in this episode, though it will be later in Lk 2:32.
Here the point of view is limited to the Jewish world. Apart from Acts
15:14 and 18:10, Luke's use of the word *laos* (people) in the singular
always refers to the Jews. Moreover, the normal reference of the
phrase 'all the people' is to the Jews (Lk 3:21; 7:29, etc.). This appears
to be the meaning in the present text as well. The 'good news' of
Lk 2:10 seems to echo the 'good news' of peace and God's kingship
found in Isa 52:7, as well as the 'good news' of the Lord's anointed
in Isa 61:1.

Lk 2:11 is cast in the format of an imperial proclamation,
affirming that Jesus, not the emperor Augustus, was the Saviour and
source of peace whose birthday, 'this day', marked a new beginning of
time. The Old Testament background for this verse is probably Isa
9:6(5), 'For to us a child is born, to us a son is given'.

The angel announces the birth of the Messiah 'in the city of
David'. In the Old Testament, the title 'city of David' was given to the
mountain of Zion, in Jerusalem, the residence of David. We have here
in Lk 2:11 a typically Christian appellation for Bethlehem, the city
where the 'son of David' was to be born according to the prophecy of
Micah (5:2–4[1–3]):

5:2(1) But you, O Bethlehem Ephrathah,
        who are little to be among the clans of Judah,
        from you shall come forth for me
        one who is to be ruler in Israel,
        whose origin is from of old,
        from ancient days.

5:3(2) Therefore he shall give them up until the time
        when she who is in travail has brought forth;
        then the rest of his brethren shall return
        to the people of Israel.

5:4(3)   And he shall stand and feed his flock
         in the strength of the Lord,
         in the majesty of the name of the Lord his God.

The prophecy of Micah is realized: 'Today' is born. . . . 'Today' has, in Luke, a particular ring of eschatological realization of the redemption. Compare Lk 4:21, 'Today this scripture has been fulfilled in your hearing'; Lk 19:9, 'Today salvation has come to this house'; Lk 23:43, 'Today you will be with me in Paradise'. Not in some future time, but at that very moment, a Saviour makes his appearance. This use of 'today' also reminds us of the Old Testament enthronement or exaltation formula in Ps 2:7, 'You are my son, today I have begotten you'.

The titles given to Jesus are to be explained by the same Davidic messianism. 'Christ the Lord' (*Christos Kurios*) has its foundation in the Old Testament where the Messiah is often called Lord, e.g., Ps 110(109):1, 'The Lord (*Yahweh*) says to my lord (*Messiah*): Sit at my right hand'. The title 'Saviour' (*Sōtēr*) is a divine attribute and is seldom used to speak of the Messiah. If a Hebrew original for this passage is accepted, this term must be taken as an allusion to the name *Jesus*. To his Greek readers, Matthew explained the etymology: 'and you shall call his name Jesus, for he will save his people from their sins' (Mt 1:21). In Hebrew such an explanation would be completely superfluous; the root 'save' (*yashah*) is the same as the root of the name Jesus. Luke, it is interesting to note, seems to be the only New Testament author who juxtaposes the terms 'Christ' and 'Lord' in designating Jesus. However, Phil 3:20 applies the three titles found in Lk 2:11 to the Jesus of the parousia: 'But our commonwealth is in heaven, and from it we await a Saviour, the Lord Jesus Christ'.

Verse 12: 'And this will be a sign for you: you will find a babe wrapped in swaddling cloths and lying in a manger.'

The second reference to the manger is far more significant than that of Lk 2:7, for it is explicitly related to the notion of 'sign'. The message to the shepherds and the whole people of Israel is supported by the sign that they 'will find a babe wrapped in swaddling cloths and lying in a manger'. The condition in which the child is found is related to the previous statement that he is 'a Saviour, who is Christ the Lord' (Lk 2:11). The sign of Lk 2:12 seems to have something to do with the person of the Messiah and his role in God's saving intervention. The function of the sign is not merely to authenticate the preceding statements, but rather to explain and bring to the fore the message announced by the angels. Both message and sign should make us understand the divine will as expressed in the scriptures.

The term 'sign' (*sēmeion*) is frequently used in biblical texts whose formulation is very similar to that of Lk 2:12. This provides a reliable basis for the opinion which sees in Luke's text more than a simple affirmation of the angel's truthfulness. The sign is intimately related to the preceding message and clearly exemplifies or develops it, thus helping us to understand the message better, and contributing to its realization. Now, in the present sign, we find two important features which correspond to elements in the preceding message. First, the sign concentrates on *the child and his condition*. The circumstances in which the child is to be found, that is, 'wrapped in swaddling cloths and lying in a manger', are especially meaningful. Secondly, the sign involves the *people* to whom it is given. They are told: 'you will find. . . .'. Their *finding* the child in particular circumstances is clearly also of great importance. Indeed, the sign comprises not only the child in the manger, but also the fact of their finding him there.

In both sign and message, there seems to be a relationship between the child and the people: in the message, the child's titles 'Saviour' and 'Christ the Lord', are announced to them; in the sign, he is found by them in special circumstances, 'wrapped in swaddling clothes and lying in a manger'. The child's situation and their finding of the child in this situation indicate God's new disposition toward his people. This disposition is expressed in both the titles and the accompanying sign.

Verses 13–14: And suddenly there was with the angel a multitude of the heavenly host praising God and saying, (14) 'Glory to God in the highest, and on earth peace among men with whom he is pleased!'

God's new disposition is further expressed in the praise of the 'multitude of the heavenly host'. The multitude may recall Dan 7:10, 'a thousand thousands served him, and ten thousand times ten thousand stood before him'. In the Old Testament the expression 'heavenly host' sometimes indicates heavenly bodies. See Jer 19:13, 'all the house upon whose roofs incense has been burned to all the host of heaven'. In some later Old Testament books the phrase was used of angels associated with these heavenly bodies. Speaking of the creation, the Book of Job says: 'when the morning stars sang together, and all the sons of God (= angels) shouted for joy' (Job 38:7). So now the same chorus gathers 'praising God' for the new creation, in which 'his glory' will be displayed by the fulfilment of his eternal plan, and man's true 'peace' realized by the establishment of God's kingdom.

'Glory to God in the highest, and on earth peace among men with whom he is pleased!' 'Glory' means the experience and recognition of God's presence and powerful action in man's behalf. The angels speak of God's glory 'in the highest', that is, among the 'heavenly host'. 'On earth', then, forms a contrast to 'in the highest'.

Lk 2:14 can be arranged in two parallel lines, whose parallelism is, however, imperfect, for the second line is longer:

Glory (A) *to God* (B) *in the highest* (C),
and *on earth* (C) *peace* (A) *among men* (B) with whom he is pleased.

In Luke-Acts the closest parallel to the *Gloria* is the acclamation at the entry of Jesus into Jerusalem, where only in Luke's version do the multitudes praise the king who comes in the name of the Lord by shouting: 'Peace in heaven and glory in the highest!' (Lk 19:38). It has also been pointed out that Lk 2:14 seems to echo the beginning and concluding lines of the *Benedictus*:

Lk 1:68, 79	Lk 2:14
Blessed be the Lord God of Israel . . . to guide our feet into the way of peace.	Glory to God in the highest, and on earth peace among men with whom he is pleased.

'Peace' does not just mean absence of war or trouble. It stands for everything which makes for man's highest good. It refers to a situation of well-being from which all in the community (equally) benefit. Here it means that God seeks to establish a loving relationship between himself and his people. According to Isa 59:9–10, the way of peace is inseparable from justice. When justice is perverted and the rights of people violated, there is no peace (Jer 6:14).

The words 'among men' do not, directly at least, refer to interpersonal or international relationships, but to people as the recipients of God's gracious gifts. The concluding phrase, 'with whom he is pleased', does not mean that God is pleased with men because of their virtuous life or merits. Most scholars agree that 'good pleasure' (*eudokias*) must refer to God and not to man. It expresses God's will in *electing* man rather than his pleasure in man's goodness.

Several parallels in Daniel suggest that we have here an apocalyptic feature. When, in the Book of Daniel, the angel Gabriel appears to communicate a deeper understanding of the preceding vision, he says 'and I have come to tell it to you, for you are greatly beloved' (Dan 9:23). And further: 'O Daniel, man greatly beloved . . .' (Dan 10:11). Again: 'O man greatly beloved, fear not . . .' (Dan 10:19). The Hebrew or Aramaic expression is very similar to Luke's 'men of good pleasure'. Since an equivalent expression is found in other apocalyptic books, e.g., the *Apocalypse of Baruch* (1:3), we may suppose that it is a typical element of apocalyptic literary form. In the Dead Sea Scrolls, too, we have both an Aramaic and Hebrew equivalent of Luke's expression.

That God's good pleasure constitutes an apocalyptic theme becomes fully clear only in the New Testament. At Jesus' baptism, the heavenly voice declares: 'You are my beloved son; with you I am well pleased' (Lk 3:22). In Matthew, the expression is formulated in the third person (Mt 3:17) and is repeated at the transfiguration: 'This is my beloved son, with whom I am well pleased' (Mt 17:5). With good reason the expression may be connected with the prophecy of the Servant of Yahweh (Isa 42:1) quoted in Mt 12:18: 'Behold my servant whom I have chosen, my beloved with whom my soul is well pleased'.

At his baptism Jesus is portrayed as being formally constituted Messiah: on him rests the good pleasure, the favour of the divine election. We may further suppose that the messianic people, too, are included in this election. The prophecy of the Servant of Yahweh in Second Isaiah contains a tension between the individual and the collectivity or community. The eschatological community was, as it were, included in the figure of the Servant of Yahweh.

In other Old Testament texts, God's sinless people of the endtime are also the object of God's favour (Isa 62:4; Ps 147(146):11; Ps 149:4). Moreover, all scholars accept that the descriptions of the baptism and transfiguration use apocalyptic features. Let us simply mention the opening of the heavens at the baptism and the close literary relationship between the transfiguration narrative and the Book of Daniel (Dan 10).

Verses 15–17: When the angels went away from them into heaven, the shepherds said to one another, 'Let us go over to Bethlehem and see this thing that has happened, which the Lord has made known to us.' (16) And they went with haste, and found Mary and Joseph, and the babe lying in a manger. (17) And when they saw it they made known the saying which had been told them concerning this child;

After the departure of the angels, the shepherds 'went with haste' to Bethlehem to see the sign which was given to them. Compare Lk 1:38–39: '. . . and the angel departed from her. In those days Mary rose and went with haste into the hill country.' 'To see this thing' literally reads 'to see the word (*rēma*)'. But here as well as in verse 17 (RSV: 'the saying') and 19 (RSV: 'these things'), it translates the twofold connotation of the Hebrew *dābār*, 'word, deed'. These are deeds that speak.

The shepherds found 'Mary and Joseph, and the babe lying in a manger' (Lk 2:16). In this third reference to the manger it becomes quite clear that the most important feature in the narrative is the child in the manger. The swaddling cloths mentioned on two previous occasions (Lk 2:7, 12) are here omitted. The essential feature is the manger. When the shepherds saw the sign, 'they made known the saying which had been told them concerning this child' (Lk 2:17). The narrative does not focus on the apparition of the angel. The point is what had been said concerning the child who is the Saviour, Christ the Lord: he was to be found in a manger.

Traditionally, the manger and the swaddling cloths have been understood as referring to the poverty in which Jesus chose to be born. However, this interpretation seems to depend more on late medieval piety and present-day feelings and experience than on an attempt to understand this passage from within the Bible. Solid exegesis is needed to find out what the manger, the swaddling cloths, and the inn mean in the Bible, and particularly in Luke. If we take this as a starting-point, we find that three Old Testament texts shed light on the mystery.

The first is Isa 1:3:

> The ox knows its owner,
> and the ass its master's crib (manger),
> but Israel does not know (*the Greek text adds*: me),
> my people does not understand (*the Greek text adds*: me).

Although the RSV translates 'crib', the Greek word used, *phatnē*, is the same as the word for 'manger' in Luke.

The meaning of Isa 1:3 is the following: Yahweh compares himself to Israel's owner and its source of sustenance. Israel does not know its owner and its source of sustenance, whereas the ox and the ass know their owner and know how to find the source of their sustenance: the crib or the manger.

Now in Lk 2:12 and 16, Luke says that the shepherds 'find' the child in a 'manger'. They have found again the source of their sustenance, because God has taken the initiative and has shown them the way by letting them find the child in the manger. Note also that in Isa 1:3 one finds the ox and the ass which are almost inseparable from the popular presentation of Christmas, but are not found in the infancy narratives themselves.

The second text is Jer 14:8:

> O you hope of Israel,
> its saviour in time of trouble,
> why should you be like a stranger in the land,
> like a wayfarer who turns aside to tarry for the night?

Although RSV translates 'who turns aside to tarry for the night', the Greek text of Jeremiah contains the word for 'inn' (*kataluma*) which is used by Luke. We could translate Jeremiah: 'like a wayfarer who stays in an inn for the night'. In II Sam 7:6 *kataluma* is the dwelling place of the Divine Presence in the desert journey of Israel. In I Sam 1:18 (in the Septuagint Greek) Elkanah and Hannah, the future parents of Samuel, stop at a *kataluma* at Shiloh, the holy place where Hannah's prayer for a child is answered. The latter text may have had some importance for Luke's presentation. In Lk 9:12 and 19:7 the verb *kataluein* is used for people who must unexpectedly look for lodging.

The meaning of Jer 14:8 is the following: Jeremiah complains that God has forgotten his people. He no longer 'visits' his people as his own. And when he happens to pass through the country, he does not stay with his own, but lodges in an inn as a foreign traveller would do. If the child Jesus is to be the expression of God's new disposition toward his people, he should not stay in an inn. Instead of 'there was no place for them in the inn', one could translate freely, 'the inn was not the proper place for them to stay', especially for the child.

The third text is Wis 7:4–5,

> I was nursed with care in swaddling cloths,
> for no king has had a different beginning of existence.

In this text Solomon is speaking. He says that at his birth he too was wrapped in swaddling cloths, a sign of maternal care. Solomon was a royal child, and more precisely the son of David. So, far from stressing the poverty in which Jesus was born, the swaddling cloths suggest rather that he is a royal child, a king, a son of David.

The three texts mentioned (Isa 1:3; Jer 14:8; Wis 7:4–5) are combined according to the methods of Jewish *midrash* which Luke imitates in the first two chapters of his gospel. If we realize that they are not used for the sake of the Old Testament texts, but are to be understood in the new context of the events Luke is trying to illuminate, they provide a deeper insight into the mystery of Jesus' birth. Jesus is born in Bethlehem, the city of David. He will not be found in an 'inn' like an alien who stays there for lack of relatives or friends, but in a 'manger', symbolizing God as the support and sustenance of his people. His royal origin is not contradicted by the fact that he is 'wrapped in swaddling cloths', for no king had a different beginning of existence.

When the shepherds saw the sign, 'they made known' the angel's interpretation of 'this child' (in contrast with the child of Lk 1:76?). Thus they were the first to announce the good news of Jesus' birth.

Verses 18–20: and all who heard it wondered at what the shepherds told them. (19) But Mary kept all these things, pondering them in her heart. (20) And the shepherds returned, glorifying and praising God for all they had heard and seen, as it had been told them.

Those who heard it 'wondered' (compare Lk 1:21, 63), a frequently mentioned reaction which does not necessarily express faith (see Acts 3:12, 'Men of Israel, why do you wonder at this, or why do you stare at us . . .'). It can even be explicitly connected with unbelief (see Lk 24:41, 'And while they disbelieved for joy, and wondered . . .').

After the account of the visit of the shepherds and the amazement of those hearing their story, Luke reports that 'Mary kept all these things, pondering them in her heart'. The same remark is reiterated at the end of the infancy narrative (Lk 2:51). Did the author intend to allude to information about Jesus' birth and youth given by Mary herself? Or did he draw our attention to the piety of Mary who *meditated upon* these things in her heart? Too often these explanations are taken for granted without sufficient effort to understand the wealth of meaning contained in this verse.

The initial 'but' expresses a contrast between 'all who heard' and were (merely) amazed, and Mary who alone retained what was heard. The others were like 'those who, when they hear the word, receive it with joy; but these have no root . . .' (Lk 8:13), while Mary is one of 'those who, hearing the word, hold it fast in an honest and good heart' (Lk 8:15). It can hardly be accidental that in the only scene in which Mary appears during Jesus' ministry and which occurs only four verses later (Lk 8:19–21), Jesus says: 'my mother and my brothers are those who hear the word of God and do it' (Lk 8:21).

In Semitic anthropology, the 'heart' plays an extremely important role: it is the seat not so much of affections and sentiments, as of the will and intelligence. In many texts the activities of the spirit are ascribed to the heart. After Zechariah, at the giving of the name, recovered his speech, it is said in Lk 1:66, 'all who heard them laid them up in their hearts'.

In apocalyptic literature, 'to treasure the words in one's heart' is a frequently occurring formula found in characteristic texts. At the end of the chapter dealing with the vision of 'one like a son of man', Daniel declares, 'I kept the matter in my mind' (Dan 7:28; literally, 'I kept the word in my heart'). In Dan 8:26, Daniel receives the command to put a seal on the vision, 'for it pertains to many days hence', and the same command is repeated in Dan 12:4, 9. The same ideas are found in apocryphal apocalypses.

From all this it follows that the expression 'to treasure the words in one's heart' belongs to the apocalyptic themes and that it was in current use as an almost technical formula after a vision, frequently a vision concerning the enthronement of the Messiah. The 'word' or 'words' are nothing else than the vision itself which preceded, and which is to be kept and treasured till the time of its fulfilment.

The formula is also found in the New Testament. The Book of Revelation (Apocalypse of John) opens with the words: 'and blessed are those who hear, and who keep what is written therein; for the time is near' (Rev 1:3). And the same book concludes with the remark: 'Blessed is he who keeps (= treasures) the words of the prophecy of this book' (Rev 22:7). The time of fulfilment is near: 'Do not seal up the words of the prophecy of this book, for the time is near' (Rev 22:10).

This apocalyptic theme is also found in the gospels. After the confession of Peter, Jesus commands his disciples to keep it a secret (Lk 9:21 and parallels). We are indeed in a truly apocalyptic context: 'Blessed are you, Simon Bar-Jona! For flesh and blood has not revealed this to you, but my Father who is in heaven' (Mt 16:17). This revelation of the Son by the Father reminds us of Gal 1:15–16 which deals with Paul's vocation to become the apostle of the Gentiles. In Mt 16:17, it is Peter who, on the basis of a revelation, is constituted a foundation of the Church. The idea of Church, like the transcendent figure of the son of man in Daniel, places the passage in the apocalyptic context of Daniel 7: the vision of the son of man and the people, the saints of the Most High who receive the kingdom.

The account of the transfiguration is closely related to the confession of Peter. Here the transcendence of Jesus is once again revealed, this time in a manifestation described according to the literary model of Dan 10. The disciples must keep this apocalyptic vision a secret: 'Tell no one the vision, until the Son of man is raised from the dead' (Mt 17:9). Only Mark notes further that they did keep the vision a secret: 'so they kept the matter to themselves, questioning what the rising from the dead meant' (Mk 9:10).

Studying the theme 'to treasure the words' helps us to discover the apocalyptic character of the story of the shepherds. The expression is, however, repeated at the end of the infancy narrative. In Lk 2:51, the expression refers to the whole account and not, as is often said, only to the immediately preceding episode, particularly the 'word' of Jesus concerning his 'Father's house' (Lk 2:49) which his parents did not understand (Lk 2:50).

So Mary's response is described in terms very close to those used in Dan 7:28. Similarly Jacob 'kept the saying in mind' and pondered the significance of Joseph's dreams (Gen 37:11). It is not yet clear how God's purpose will be realized. To receive a vision is not always to understand its realization in the practical circumstances of everyday life. But in Lk 1:45 Mary is presented as a model for the believing community. Faithful hearing and keeping of God's word is a recurrent theme in Luke's gospel (see Lk 8:15, 19–21; 10:39; 11:28).

Lk 2:20 concludes the present episode with the literary device of *leave-taking*. The shepherds returned to their flocks, 'glorifying and praising God'. Joyful thanksgiving is one of Luke's favourite themes (*doxazō* is found fourteen times in Luke-Acts, against once in Mark and four times in Matthew).

The naming and manifestation of Jesus (Lk 2:21–40)

The circumcision and naming of Jesus (Lk 2:21) and the presentation of Jesus in the Temple (Lk 2:22–24) introduce the core of the passage, the inspired testimony of Simeon and Anna (Lk 2:25–38). Simeon is the recipient of three specific interventions of the Spirit: (1) it is revealed to him that he will live to 'see' the Messiah (Lk 2:26); (2) in Jesus he recognizes the fulfilment of the promise; and (3) he pronounces the *Nunc Dimittis* which, in the context, is to be considered as a prophetic prayer (Lk 2:29–32). Anna does not utter any prophecy, but 'she gave thanks to God', and it is implied that this thanksgiving is inspired by her prophetic knowledge of Jesus' Messiahship (Lk 2:38). The episode is concluded with a *leave-taking* (Lk 2:39) and a *refrain of growth* (Lk 2:40).

> **Verse 21:** And at the end of eight days, when he was circumcised, he was called Jesus, the name given by the angel before he was conceived in the womb.

Literally the text reads: 'when the eight days were fulfilled to circumcise the child'. The expression 'the days were fulfilled' occurs also for Jesus' birth (Lk 2:6) and the purification (Lk 2:22). This is Luke's way of connecting the three events of the birth, circumcision, and purification. The circumcision and naming of Jesus are parallel to Lk 1:59–63, the circumcision of John. Again Luke emphasizes the giving of the name. It was the father's right to name the child (Lk 1:62). As in the case of John, the heavenly Father has again bestowed the name through the agency of the angel Gabriel (Lk 1:31). Since the name is not just a label but tells us what a person is like, to be named by God before birth is of great importance. For Luke and Matthew (Mt 1:21) it expresses the nature of Jesus' mission. The name Jesus means 'Yahweh saves'.

> **Verses 22–24:** And when the time came for their purification according to the law of Moses, they brought him up to Jerusalem to present him to the Lord (23) (as it is written in the law of the Lord, 'Every male that opens the womb shall be called holy to the Lord') (24) and to offer a sacrifice according to what is said in the law of the Lord, 'a pair of turtle-doves, or two young pigeons.'

According to Lev 12:2–4, after the birth of a son the mother was unclean for seven days, until the circumcision, and the period of purification then continued for another thirty-three days. The purification was purely ritual in character and did not imply any moral fault in sexual relations and childbirth. After the forty days of purification were over, the mother was to bring her offering to the priest in the sanctuary.

The purification ceremony is here combined with the requirement of consecration of the first-born to the Lord (Ex 13:2, 12). Originally the eldest son was dedicated to the service of God, but since the tribe of Levi had been set apart for that purpose, the first-born in other tribes could be 'redeemed' or 'ransomed' through the payment of a nominal price to the priest (Num 18:15f.).

As can easily be seen from the text, one of the motifs of Lk 2:22–24 (and indeed of the whole of Lk 2:22–40) is that both the law and the prophets are fulfilled in Jesus.

In recent years scholars have stressed the importance of the city of Jerusalem for the theology of Luke. This applies also to the infancy narrative, but the full meaning of this conclusion for Lk 1 – 2 has not yet been developed. The importance given to Jerusalem in these chapters (Lk 2:22, 25, 38, 41, 43, 45) is the more striking if we contrast it with Matthew's treatment of the infancy narrative, in which Jerusalem is mentioned only once (Mt 2:3), and which describes Jesus' infancy in such a way that he is completely dissociated from that city. It is fairly generally accepted that for theological reasons Luke transferred the location of the resurrection appearances from Galilee to Jerusalem. Should a theological importance then not be attached to Luke's emphasis on Jerusalem in the infancy narrative? Luke develops this theme especially in the presentation of Jesus in the Temple (Lk 2:22–40) where we are told that 'they brought him up to Jerusalem to present him to the Lord' (Lk 2:22). It is worth noting that in this episode several implications of Jesus' coming into the world, especially the universality of salvation (Lk 2:31–32), are already expressed.

It is nowhere legislated that the child should be presented at the *Temple*, yet the fact that Jesus was so presented seems to be of great importance for Luke. He may have thought of the dedication of Samuel at the temple of Shiloh (I Sam 1:11, 22–28). One could also refer to Malachi 3. Since John the Baptist has been presented as the messenger, who will prepare the way of the Lord (Mal 3:1, 4:5[3:23]; Lk 1:17, 76), we may suppose that the one who is now presented at the Temple is the Lord himself: 'Behold, I send my messenger to prepare the way before me, and the Lord whom you seek will suddenly come to his temple' (Mal 3:1).

'Every male that opens the womb shall be called holy to the Lord.' This refers to the presentation of the first-born as prescribed in Ex 13:2, 12, 15, but the word 'holy' is here, as in Lk 1:35, inserted by Luke, most probably under the influence of Dan 9:24, which tells us of the consecration of a 'Holy One' at the inauguration of the messianic age.

Mary offered 'two young pigeons'. The regulations for this

sacrifice are found in Lev 12. The normal sacrifice was a lamb a year old and a young pigeon or a turtledove (Lev 12:6); but the regulations go on: 'And if she cannot afford a lamb, she shall take two turtledoves or two young pigeons' (Lev 12:8). This sacrifice was known as the 'offering of the poor', and although we are not certain whether the alternative offered in Leviticus was still an active custom in Jesus' time, it is worth noting that it was this offering that Mary brought.

Verses 25–28: Now there was a man in Jerusalem, whose name was Simeon, and this man was righteous and devout, looking for the consolation of Israel, and the Holy Spirit was upon him. (26) And it had been revealed to him by the Holy Spirit that he should not see death before he had seen the Lord's Christ. (27) And inspired by the Spirit he came into the temple; and when the parents brought in the child Jesus, to do for him according to the custom of the law, (28) he took him up in his arms and blessed God and said:

It was an ancient Jerusalem custom for parents to bring their child to the Temple and to request a rabbi to bless it. It was most probably for this purpose that Jesus was placed in the arms of Simeon. The Old Testament background for the Simeon (and Anna) story is taken from I Sam 1 – 2, concerning the figures of Eli, the priest, and Hannah, the mother of Samuel.

Simeon was 'righteous and devout', earnestly concerned with the realization of God's will, and he was 'looking for the consolation of Israel', a typical rabbinic expression for the Messiah or the messianic age. The idea can be traced to the initial words of Second Isaiah (Isa 40 – 55), also called the Book of Consolation. In fact, the *Nunc Dimittis* is very much indebted to these prophecies. Like Simeon, Joseph of Arimathea was 'a good and righteous man . . . looking for the kingdom of God' (Lk 23:50–51). And the people to whom Anna addressed her message are described as 'all who were looking for the redemption of Jerusalem' (Lk 2:38). Simeon and Anna are the embodiment of the piety of the *anawim* (see above, Chapter Six, commentary on the *Magnificat*).

'The Holy Spirit was upon him' means that God gave him the *power* to understand the importance of what was happening at that moment of Israel's history. Note the thrice-repeated reference to the 'Holy Spirit'. Luke is the gospel of the Holy Spirit (Lk 1:15; 1:35; 1:41; 1:67; 2:25; 2:26; 2:27, etc.). It is also clear that what Simeon was about to say was of prophetic inspiration. The clause 'he should not see death' means 'he would not experience death'. The twice-repeated 'see' prepares for the words of the following hymn, 'for my eyes have seen your salvation' (Lk 2:30).

Verses 29–32: 'Lord, now you let your servant depart in peace, according to your word;
(30)   for my eyes have seen your salvation
(31)   which you have prepared in the presence of all peoples,
(32)   a light for revelation to the Gentiles, and for glory to your people Israel.'

The *Nunc Dimittis* is the third canticle which is proper to Luke. The Greek word rendered 'Lord' (*despota*) is found only here in Lk 2:29 and Acts 4:24 in Luke's two-volume work. In Acts 4:24 it appears in the prayer of the Christian community at Jerusalem which may very well have been the source of this hymn (as well as of the *Benedictus* and *Magnificat*?). The word *despota* is also found in Dan 9:8, 16, 17, 19. It is best translated 'Master' and is an appropriate counterpart for Simeon's self-designation as 'servant' (*doulos*, better: 'slave'). Likewise Mary is called a 'handmaiden' (*doulē*) in the *Magnificat* (Lk 1:48).

The phrase 'in peace' reminds us of Lk 1:79; 2:14. It had been revealed to Simeon that he would not die before he had seen the Messiah. Because this has now been fulfilled ('according to your word'), Simeon can 'depart in peace'. In Lk 2:30 the deeper ground for Simeon's words about peace is revealed. Throughout the Old Testament salvation was the object of a promise, but according to Isa 40:5 (quoted in Lk 3:6) it would one day reach its fulfilment and be seen, that is, experienced or shared. The *Nunc Dimittis* goes beyond the *Benedictus* in that the salvation mentioned in Lk 1:69–71, 77 is now identified with Jesus.

The opening lines of the *Nunc Dimittis* remind one of Gen 15:15, where God promises Abraham, 'you shall go to your fathers in peace', as well as Gen 46:30, the statement made by Jacob on finding his long-lost son Joseph, 'Now let me die, since I have seen your face'.

God has prepared his salvation 'in the presence of all peoples'. Compare Isa 52:10, 'The Lord has bared his holy arm before the eyes of all the nations; and all the ends of the earth shall see the salvation of our God', and Ps 98(97):2, 'The Lord has made known his victory, he has revealed his vindication in the sight of the nations'. But note that these two texts, in accordance with the Greek version of Isaiah and the Psalms, use the term 'nations', that is, Gentiles, and not 'peoples' as in Lk 2:31. The shift from 'nations' to 'peoples' may be explained by one of Luke's major theological interests, that the good news is addressed to all nations via the people of Israel. The Gentiles, therefore, are also called to belong to God's people, and it is probable that 'all peoples' refers to both Jews and Gentiles.

In Lk 2:32 the phrase 'all peoples' is divided into two separate groups: Gentiles and Israel. God's salvation is to be 'a light for revelation to the Gentiles'. Ps 98(97):2, combined with Isa 40:5, 'all flesh shall see it together', and Isa 49:6, 'I will give you as a light to the nations, that my salvation may reach to the end of the earth', shed light on the meaning of this verse. Alluding to Ps 98(97):3, the *Magnificat* (Lk 1:54) limited the promise to Israel. Here, alluding to the same context, Ps 98(97):2, Lk 2:32 includes the Gentiles as recipients of the light announced by Zechariah in the *Benedictus* (Lk 1:78–79). Attempts to deny a universalistic perspective to Lk 2:30–32 prove unconvincing. In the prophetic words of Simeon Luke anticipates what he will describe in the Acts of the Apostles. With his keen sense for the different periods in the unfolding of God's plan of salvation, Luke places the fulfilment of this prophecy not in Jesus' earthly ministry, but in the period of the post-Pentecostal Church. In Acts 15:14 James says that '*Simeon* (Peter) has related how God first visited the Gentiles, to take out of them a people for his name'. This action related by Peter reaches its conclusion at the end of Acts 28:28 when Paul says, 'Let it be known to you then that this salvation of God has been sent to the Gentiles'. At this point the vision of Simeon at the presentation of Jesus in the Temple is verified.

'And for the glory of your people Israel.' The concluding words of the *Nunc Dimittis* seem to be inspired by Isa 46:13, 'I bring near my deliverance, it is not far off, and my salvation will not tarry; I will put salvation in Zion, for Israel my glory'. Jesus is God's final and decisive revelation to Israel. In and through him Israel can reach its ultimate goal as people of God. Therefore, Jesus is called its 'glory'.

> **Verses 33–35:** And his father and mother marvelled at what was said about him; (34) and Simeon blessed them and said to Mary his mother, 'Behold, this child is set for the fall and rising of many in Israel, and for a sign that is spoken against (35) (and a sword will pierce through your own soul also), that thoughts out of many hearts may be revealed.'

Notwithstanding Gabriel's message (Lk 1:31–35) and the words of the shepherds (Lk 2:17) 'his father and mother marvelled', that is, they reacted with surprise and perplexity to all that had been said concerning the child (compare Lk 1:29; 2:18).

Simeon invokes a blessing on the parents and then addresses Mary. Her child will be the point of decision for Israel and a sign of contradiction that will reveal the secret disposition of many hearts. Incidentally, he will also cause considerable suffering to his mother.

The clause 'this child is set for the rise and fall of many' is a form of the building-stone image found repeatedly in the New Testament in connection with the mixed fate of the Jews. It can be a stone on which people stumble and fall (Isa 8:14) or it can be a cornerstone for a house (Ps 118[117]:22; Isa 28:16). It is precisely this combination of texts which concludes the parable of the vineyard which is taken from its present tenants and given to others (see Lk 20:17–18). That Jesus is called a 'sign' echoes Isa 7:14 where the child that is announced is a *sign* given to the house of David. The place where Israel 'contradicted' God during the Exodus was called the 'waters of Meribah' (Num 20:13; Deut 32:51), which means 'contradiction, contention'. Simeon prophesies that the people will contradict God again, thereby anticipating the rejection of Jesus by the Jewish authorities during his mission and passion, and the rejection of the Christian mission to Israel as described in Acts.

The clause 'a sword will pierce your own soul also' is usually interpreted as the sorrow of Mary at the foot of the cross. This explanation, however, is not satisfactory, because it limits the sense of the words to Mary alone and restricts their application to Calvary. In order to understand the verse correctly, one must start from the fact that the evangelists, and particularly Luke in chapters 1 – 2, are greatly influenced by the Old Testament. The *Nunc Dimittis* is above all inspired by Isaiah; so also Lk 2:34 (see Isa 8:14–15, 'And he will become a sanctuary, and a stone of offence, and a rock of stumbling. . . . And many shall stumble thereon; they shall fall and be broken . . .'). The reason why the Messiah will be a sign of contradiction is that he falls short of the national longings of the Jews and that he will be a light for the Gentiles (Isa 49:6).

The metaphor of the sword seems to be taken from the same context, namely from Isa 49:2, 'He made my mouth like a sharp sword'. What Jesus himself says about his mission confirms this notion. He has come not to bring peace but the sword and division (Lk 12:51–53; Mt 10:34–37). On the other hand, the word of God is often compared to a sword, especially in Heb 4:12–13, 'For the word of God is living and active, sharper than any two-edged sword, piercing to the division of soul and spirit, of joints and marrow, and discerning the thoughts and intentions of the heart. . .'. Lk 2:35 shows much similarity to this text of Hebrews: in both, the sword pierces the soul, sifts the thoughts and brings them to light. A further element of explanation may be found in Ez 14:17, 'Or if I bring a sword upon that land, and say, Let a sword go through the land; and I cut off from it man and beast'. This verse describes the sword of God going through the land as a punishing force. As a symbol of division and internal contradiction, the sword occurs also in the *Sibylline Oracles* and in several biblical texts. It seems, then, that in Luke's mind the sword that will divide Israel is Jesus' revealing word. This results in salvation but also in judgment.

Some of that division and struggle will be in Mary herself. She is portrayed as the daughter of Zion who personifies the land, or better, the messianic community, and her sorrow is that of the Woman who bears in her heart the destiny of the entire chosen people, in fact of the whole human race. But it seems that Lk 2:35 means that the words of Jesus would also be a sword for Mary personally. Thus the verse means that the teaching of Jesus (Lk 12:51–53) would make Mary realize that she should give away her son to all people, should completely separate herself from him. This realization was for her a sword piercing her soul, but she accepted it and had then to learn the implications of her complete surrender to God's salvific will. Did Luke understand the following pericope (Lk 2:41–50) as a first experience of this?

In all thirteen instances where the word *dialogismos*, 'thought', occurs in the New Testament, it is used in a pejorative sense: bad thoughts, vain thoughts, doubting thoughts. In the five other instances where it occurs in Luke it means thoughts hostile to Jesus or questioning him. Here it implies that the contradiction mentioned in verse 34 is expressed in hostile thoughts. One may refer here to Lk 12:1–2 where, speaking of the hostile thought of the Pharisees, Jesus says that 'Nothing is covered up that will not be revealed, or hidden that will not be known'.

Verses 36–38: And there was a prophetess, Anna, the daughter of Phanuel, of the tribe of Asher; she was of a great age, having lived with her husband seven years from her virginity, (37) and as a widow till she was eighty-four. She did not depart from the temple, worshipping with fasting and prayer night and day. (38) And coming up at that very hour she gave thanks to God, and spoke of him to all who were looking for the redemption of Jerusalem.

Simeon's prophecy is followed by the thanksgiving of Anna. By placing Anna side-by-side with Simeon, Luke is again anticipating the Acts, more particularly Pentecost: 'And in the last days it shall be, God declares, that I will pour out my Spirit upon all flesh, and your sons and daughters shall prophesy' (Acts 2:17). As a widow, Anna dedicated her life to fasting and prayer to such an extent that she practically lived in the Temple. Striking similarities have been noted to the portrayal of Judith (Jud 8:4–8; 16:22–23). The most detailed description of Christian widows found in I Tim 5:3–16 contains many features which match Luke's description of Anna. Anna recognized the Messiah and 'spoke of him to all who were looking for the redemption of Jerusalem', that is, of Israel. Compare Isa 52:9, 'Break forth together into singing, you waste places of Jerusalem; for the Lord has comforted his people, he has redeemed Jerusalem'. Jesus' entry into the Temple constitutes the beginning of the redemption of Jerusalem or Israel from all its enemies (Lk 1:68, 71). He himself is its redeemer (Lk 24:21).

In Lk 2:21–40 the two characteristic aspects of Jesus' mission are prefigured: contradiction and acceptance, judgment and salvation, fall and resurrection. In this visit to the Temple, the prophecy of Malachi was fulfilled: 'The Lord whom you seek will suddenly come to his temple; the messenger of the covenant in whom you delight, behold, he is coming' (Mal 3:1). This coming is a day of judgment: 'But who can endure the day of his coming, and who can stand when he appears?' (Mal 3:2). But it is also a day of salvation: 'Then the offering of Judah and Jerusalem will be pleasing to the Lord as in the days of old and as in former years' (Mal 3:4).

> **Verses 39–40:** And when they had performed everything according to the law of the Lord, they returned into Galilee, to their own city, Nazareth. (40) And the child grew and became strong, filled with wisdom; and the favour of God was upon him.

These verses constitute a twofold conclusion. Verse 39 concludes the scene of the purification and presentation. Verse 39a, 'and when they had performed everything according to the law of the Lord', forms an inclusion with Lk 2:22–24 and is part of the presentation scene. It is combined with verse 39b, 'they returned into Galilee, to their own city, Nazareth'. The same combination of motifs is found in I Sam 2:20. Verse 40, which in the context of Luke's diptych pattern is parallel to Lk 1:80, was most probably the earlier conclusion of the infancy narrative, Lk 2:41–52 being almost certainly a later addition. It recalls I Sam 2:21b, 'And the boy Samuel grew in the presence of the Lord', and I Sam 2:26, 'Now the boy Samuel continued to grow both in stature and in favour with the Lord and with men'. Thus the twofold conclusion of the infancy narrative reflects the story of Samuel.

Jesus was 'filled with wisdom'. Compare Wis 7:7, 'I called upon God, and the spirit of wisdom came to me'. The next episode will give an example of this growth in wisdom as well as of the way in which Mary started to learn how she should separate herself from her son. While at an earlier stage of the composition of the infancy narrative, verse 40 may have constituted a transition to the description of Jesus' ministry (Lk 3:1) when he 'was about thirty years of age' (Lk 3:23), the insertion of Lk 2:41–52 transformed it into a transition to the present story 'when he was twelve years old' (Lk 2:42).

Jesus in the Temple (Lk 2:41–52)

Lk 2:41–52 is not the fulfilment of anything that precedes, nor does it depend for its intelligibility on what precedes in Lk 1:5 – 2:40. In fact, it can scarcely be called a section of the *infancy* narrative, since Jesus is already twelve years old. In both content and tone it is closer to the stories about the 'hidden life' of Jesus found in the apocryphal gospels of the following centuries, the best example of which is the second-century *Infancy Gospel of Thomas* which, despite its title, treats of Jesus' youth.

Within ch. 2 itself, the story in 2:41–51 is quite separable from the rest. Not only does it deal with a different phase of Jesus' life, but in its emphasis on the parents' lack of understanding (2:48–50) it seems to clash with the revelation given to them in what has gone before. One could argue that 2:40 was the original conclusion and that a story of different provenance was added, requiring a second and duplicate conclusion in 2:52.[27]

Thus it is not clear how the episode in Lk 2:41–52 is to be related to the whole of Lk 1 – 2, but it may be said with certainty that an important reason for including the incident was its setting in the Temple of Jerusalem, the place which continues to figure largely in the schema of redemption, even in the early Church. It is quite significant that later 'the things (house) of my Father' bring Jesus back to the same city, and to the same Temple (Lk 19:45).

A form-critical analysis indicates that Lk 2:41–51a was originally an isolated story which has been placed into the context of Lk 2 with obvious editorial seams. Verses 40 and 52 form an inclusion or framework within which the pericope retains its own integrity. In the early Christian tradition, and more specifically in the catechesis of the early Church, the pericope has taken on the form of a pronouncement story which reaches its climax in the pronouncement of Jesus: 'Did you not know that I must be in my Father's house?' (Lk 2:49).

Verses 41–45: Now his parents went to Jerusalem every year at the feast of the Passover. (42) And when he was twelve years old, they went up according to custom; (43) and when the feast was ended, as they were returning, the boy Jesus stayed behind in Jerusalem. His parents did not know it, (44) but supposing him to be in the company they went a day's journey, and they sought him among their kinsfolk and acquaintances; (45) and when they did not find him, they returned to Jerusalem, seeking him.

While verses 41–42, which resemble the introductory verses 22–24 of the preceding scene, supply the general introduction, verses 43–45 constitute a more specific setting. At the age of twelve a Jewish boy became a *son of the law*, that is, he was considered able to take the obligations of the law upon him. Besides, according to the law, all men who had reached the age of puberty had to go on a pilgrimage to the Temple three times a year, for the three great feasts of Passover, Pentecost and Tabernacles (Ex 23:14–17; Deut 16:16f.). In practice, most people went only once a year, at the Passover. The rabbinical interpretation of the law was that a boy was not obliged to make the journey before he had completed his twelfth year and so had reached the age of thirteen, but pious parents used to take their sons with them at an earlier age.

Luke does not tell us how Jesus and his parents came to be separated in Jerusalem. Therefore, it is pointless to speculate whether Jesus' remaining was the result of an accident (his getting lost) or a deliberate act, although the continuation seems to suggest that the boy had taken the initiative. People travelled in large groups and the women and young children started ahead of the men. They met only at night, after 'a day's journey' which would represent about twenty miles (Num 11:31; I Kgs 19:4).

> **Verses 46–47:** After three days they found him in the temple, sitting among the teachers, listening to them and asking them questions; (47) and all who heard him were amazed at his understanding and his answers.

Literally the text reads: 'And it happened (*egeneto*) after three days they found him'. It marks the beginning of the main part of the account. Apparently the incident is situated in some chamber of the Temple building where, especially during feast days, the scribes met for teaching and discussion. Jesus was attending such a discussion among a group of rabbis. We should not imagine a scene in which a precocious boy dominates a group of his seniors. 'Listening and asking questions' was a current Jewish expression for a student learning from his teachers. Jesus appears as a genuine learner. But Jesus' listening and asking questions may also foreshadow his frequent involvement in debates over the law during his public ministry. Likewise the amazement which greets Jesus' understanding and his answers (Lk 2:47) anticipates the astonishment caused by Jesus' teaching at the beginning of his ministry (Lk 4:32), and the amazement of the scribes at his answers (Lk 20:26).

'Understanding' (*sunesis*) is not necessarily of a religious nature, as can be seen, for instance, in Acts 13:7 where it is used of Sergius Paulus, the Roman proconsul of Paphos. It implies insight rather than knowledge. As such Luke considers it an example of the wisdom which he emphasizes in Lk 2:40, 52. In I Chron 22:12 David prays that God will give Solomon 'wisdom' (RSV: 'discretion') and 'understanding'. Isa 11:2 says that 'the spirit of wisdom and understanding' will rest on the king. In Lk 2:20 we were told that Jesus was 'filled with wisdom'. The author of Wisdom stated: 'Because of her (Wisdom) I shall have glory among the multitudes and honour in the presence of the elders, though I am young' (Wis 8:10). In Lk 11:31 we will be told that a greater one than Solomon is here. This theme may already underlie this pericope.

'After three days' the parents found him sitting among the doctors of the law. It is not altogether clear how we should understand the phrase 'after three days'. It may mean an unexpectedly long time. There does not seem to be any reference to the resurrection here, since, in the context of the resurrection narratives, Luke never uses the expression 'after three days', but always 'on the third day'.

> **Verses 48–50:** And when they saw him they were astonished; and his mother said to him, 'Son, why have you treated us so? Behold, your father and I have been looking for you anxiously.' (49) And he said to them, 'How is it that you sought me? Did you not know that I must be in my Father's house?' (50) And they did not understand the saying which he spoke to them.

Mary's reproach, 'why have you treated us so?' is similar in form to phrases found in the Septuagint (e.g., Gen 12:18; 20:9; 26:10; 29:25; Ex 14:11; Num 23:11; Judg 15:11). In these Old Testament passages the phrase connotes disappointment in response to some deceptive or disillusioning action. In contrast to the customary Old Testament word for 'that' (*touto*), which mostly refers to the action prompting the disappointment, Luke instead uses the Greek word for 'so' or 'thus' (*houtōs*). This seems to be a deliberate alteration of a formula, consciously adopted by Luke, who thereby avoids the suggestion that Jesus' activity in the Temple is under criticism. Instead the formula now prepares the way for the claim pronounced in verse 49, which in turn defines the impropriety of the parents' disappointment.

Jesus, indeed, does not answer Mary on the same level. We can translate either 'about my Father's affairs' or 'in my Father's house'. The phrase 'I must' (Greek: *dei*) expresses a sense of vocation and obligation which appears often in subsequent Lucan passages in which Jesus speaks of the mission the Father has given him (Lk 4:43; 9:22; 13:32–33; 17:25; 22:37; 24:7, 26). Jesus here asserts his own personal duty to his Father and, in the interests of that duty, an absolute independence of creatures, including his mother, who 'did not understand what he meant'. Jesus' mission will break the natural family ties (see Mk 3:31–35). Jesus' attitude toward Mary in Lk 2:48–50 is an anticipation of his attitude toward her in his ministry.

> The center of the story is not the boy's intelligence but his reference to God as his Father in vs. 49. . . . The present setting and saying are no less and no more historical than are the divine voice and its setting at the baptism of Jesus. . . . And so . . . one must desist from using the present scene to establish a historical development (or lack of development) in Jesus' self-awareness. It is not possible to argue from vs. 49 that Jesus as a boy knew he was the Son of God. It is equally impossible to argue from vs. 52 (which is a standard description of growth) that Jesus grew in human knowledge.[28]

The phrase 'they did not understand', which refers – notwithstanding a great deal of wishful speculation which tries to avoid this obvious conclusion – to the real lack of understanding of Mary and Joseph, draws a sharp contrast between the parents' lack of understanding and Jesus' understanding (Lk 2:47). Their lack of understanding concerns Jesus' statement in verse 49. To a mother who came speaking of 'your father and I' Jesus replied by insisting on the priority of another Father's demands, but his earthly parents did not understand. Some of Jesus' statements about his mission meet the same kind of misunderstanding (Lk 4:22).

> **Verses 51–52:** And he went down with them and came to Nazareth, and was obedient to them; and his mother kept all these things in her heart. (52) And Jesus increased in wisdom and in stature, and in favour with God and man.

The time for the complete separation has not yet come, and Jesus returns with his parents to Nazareth. It is stated again that Mary pondered all these events in her heart, probably meaning in this case the whole infancy narrative. An explanation of the expression 'kept all these things in her heart' has already been given (see comment on Lk 2:19).

Verses 51–52 are a general recapitulation in which all the refrains of the narrative are once again repeated as a conclusion: departure, the conservation of words, the growth. We can no longer be astonished at the fact that the expression 'to treasure the words' appears at the end of this narrative, after having read the Book of Daniel and the Book of Revelation. This allows us to conclude that Lk 1 – 2 are rightly understood as a whole. We may expect to understand it better if we read it with the apocalyptic themes in mind. This is especially true of the narrative of the shepherds (Lk 2:8–20) which, notably because of the repetition of the expression 'to keep in one's heart' in verses 19 and 51, may be considered the centre of the infancy narrative.

Mary may have been amazed at what Jesus did; she may have reproached him (Lk 2:48); she may not have understood what he said, but she is open to the mystery which surrounds him. She keeps these events in her heart in preparation for a future understanding as a member of the post-Easter believing community (see Acts 1:14).

Verse 52 echoes Lk 2:40 and underlines the complementary character of Lk 2:41–51. It closely resembles I Sam 2:21, 26, 'And the boy Samuel grew in the presence of the Lord. . . . Now the boy Samuel continued to grow both in stature and in favour with the Lord and with men.' The son who is obedient (see Lk 2:51) is assured in Prov 3:4, 'So you will find favour and good repute (Hebrew: understanding) in the sight of God and man'. But Luke stresses again Jesus' 'wisdom'. The 'refrain of growth' once again rounds off the episode and at the same time the whole infancy narrative.

8 Preaching the Infancy Gospels

When we set out to preach the infancy narratives today we should first of all remember that they were not part of the earliest preaching of the Church. The early Christians proclaimed the death and resurrection of Christ. This was soon prefaced by a general reference to, and later by an actual selection of Jesus' words and deeds, his public ministry. Much later, Matthew and Luke added the infancy narratives as a kind of prologue. As mentioned in the general survey of the infancy narratives in Chapter One, these narratives were not considered in the early Church as an essential part of the gospel message. Otherwise Mark and John could not be called gospels in a true sense.

This leads us to a fundamental insight: the infancy narratives can be correctly understood only if we read them as composed after, and in the light of, the resurrection experience. They can be understood only in constant reference to the passion and resurrection narratives and to the continuing experience of the early Christian Church. This means also that the infancy narratives do not add anything really new to the gospel message proper.

This important consideration leads to the following general guidelines for our use of the infancy narratives in pastoral preaching and catechetical instructions.

(1) Under the influence of apocryphal gospels and medieval Nativity plays a whole set of ideas and interpretations has grown up around the infancy narratives. If we allow our preaching of the message to be conditioned by these products of devotion then we will almost certainly sink to the level of comforting emotions and so regress into a harmless world of childish imaginations. The homilist should take pains to ensure that what he says of the origins of Jesus' life conforms to the actual message of the gospel, especially the passion and resurrection. If he does so, then his sermon will not look like a summary of a Nativity play, but rather what it should always be, a proclamation of Jesus as the Lord and Saviour.

(2) If we consider the birth of Jesus in the light of Easter, then all kind of distortions will be eliminated and we will be able to see the

infancy narratives in the broader perspective of salvation history, i.e., history as guided by God. Jesus is the fulfilment of the promises; in him God's decisive intervention in history has become 'today' (Lk 2:11). Confessing our faith in him is not a private affair – as might easily be concluded from the way we usually celebrate Christmas – but a proclamation to the world.

(3) If the infancy narratives are to be understood in the light of the Easter event, which is always a present reality, then they cannot be taken merely as the record of a past reality. The early Christian communities did not intend the infancy narratives to be an historical reconstruction of the beginnings of Jesus' life, but rather an interpretation of the person and birth of Jesus in the light of their faith in the risen Christ. By their witness they invite us to believe not in an infant Messiah but in the risen Christ who is present now. This presence contains a reference to the past but is not restricted to it. Jesus is always present to us as the Christ, the Lord and Saviour (Lk 2:11). This he became in his death and resurrection (cf. Rom 1:3–4; Phil 2:8–11).

(4) The infancy narratives are a proclamation of the risen Christ. They embody the Easter faith of the early Christians. This is their real core. This same Easter faith should also be the goal of all our preaching. The preaching of the infancy narratives, therefore, should not be an attempt to retell the story as realistically as possible. This will almost inevitably lead to the inclusion of elements which are not found in the gospel text and will turn the interest of the listeners away from the real message of the text. The evangelists do not set out to give us an exact report of how Jesus was born (cf. Chapter One): they were not composing the first part of a 'life of Christ'. Rather they give us an interpretation of Jesus' birth inspired by the early Christians' confession of faith in the risen Christ. If the homilist acts as though he were retelling in his own words a precise eyewitness report of what happened, then he is misleading his hearers.

In preaching the message of the infancy narratives we should refrain from all attempts at historical reconstruction and apply ourselves to the proclamation of the living and present Christ. The homilist should first of all serve the interests of the word of God and not the expectations of his audience. In fact, he will serve his listeners today best by faithfully adhering to the authentic Christmas message of Matthew and Luke.

With these general guidelines in mind, let us now look more specifically at the individual episodes of the infancy narratives in Matthew and Luke and offer some suggestions and comments which may help to give a better basis for the manner in which we can preach them today. Much of what is said can be readily derived from the body of the book, but it is hoped readers will be helped by drawing together in this final chapter points which seem to be of more immediate pastoral importance for preaching and catechizing.

The genealogy of Jesus (Mt 1:1–17)

This text is read during the Vigil Mass of Christmas, years A, B and C, together with Mt 1:18–25, and on the Ferial of December 17.

The nature of biblical genealogies in general and a comparison with the genealogy of Lk 3:23–38 show that we cannot consider this as an exact list of Jesus' ancestors. We are dealing here rather with the shortest possible summary of the history of God's people, divided into three periods: (1) from Abraham, the very first ancestor of Israel, to the climax of the kingship of David; (2) from David to the disappearance of the kingship with the Babylonian exile; (3) from the Babylonian exile until the 'restoration' of the Davidic kingship with Jesus. This genealogy allows Matthew to situate the coming of Jesus in the history of God's dealings with his people. It focuses on the person of David (mentioned five times in verses 1–17) and therefore on the Davidic descent of Jesus. He is a 'Son of David'.

A special feature of this genealogy is the presence of the names of four women. Whatever their actual behaviour had been, they were considered by contemporary Jewish thinking as examples of eagerness to co-operate with God's design in bringing about the birth of the Messiah. This shows at the same time that God can make use even of irregularities to realize his plans.

The announcement of the birth of Jesus (Mt 1:18–25)

This pericope is read on the Fourth Sunday of Advent A and the Ferial of December 18 (Mt 1:18–24), and on the Vigil of Christmas, A, B and C, as the second part of the gospel reading, following Mt 1:1–17; part of it forms part of the alternative gospel for the Feast of St Joseph (Mt 1:16, 18–21, 24a).

First, it should be explained that Joseph and Mary were 'engaged', but not yet married, as the Jerusalem Bible's translation 'decided to divorce her informally' might make us think. Yet according to contemporary Jewish custom this engagement was considered binding. Therefore, dissolving it could be called 'divorce', just as breaking this bond unilaterally was considered 'adultery'.

It should be made clear that Joseph 'resolved to send her away quietly'. This was not because he suspected Mary of adultery or because he was ignorant of what had actually happened. Rather, knowing that her pregnancy was due to the intervention of God's Spirit in Mary's life, and 'being a just man', he did not want to be an obstacle to God's plans with Mary and so wanted to give her up and leave her free.

Through an angel, God tells Joseph that he is to have a part in God's plans and that he has to assume the *legal* fatherhood over Jesus by giving him the name which, however, has been chosen by God himself, who is, therefore, Jesus' *real* Father.

Joseph appears to us as a man who is all attention and submission to God's plans, who decided to step out of Mary's life to let God's plans materialize. When God tells him that not his solution to the problem but God's own solution has to be followed, he gives up his initial plan and takes Mary into his home.

Quoting Isa 7:14, Matthew tells us that the birth of this child will completely fulfil the promise contained in Isaiah's prophecy. This child will truly be Emmanuel, God with us.

The visit of the Magi (Mt 2:1–12)

This story is read on the Feast of the Epiphany of the Lord, A, B and C.

The brief and sober phrase, 'wise men from the East came to Jerusalem', contrasts strongly with the fantasies of popular devotion and many a sermon given on the Magi. The story mentions neither the number of wise men, nor the colour of their skin, nor their royal status, nor their caravan. The intention of the pericope is not to make the Magi the focus of interest, but to draw our attention to the whereabouts of the one 'who has been born king of the Jews'.

The homilist should not try to give a colourful picture of the Magi's journey, its hardships, or their being the laughing-stock of their countrymen. All these extraneous details, which are not in the text, turn the attention of the faithful away from the real message. Again, it is the message of the one 'who has been born king of the Jews' that constitutes the focal point of this story.

One should resist the temptation of an exaggerated symbolic interpretation of the gifts the Magi bring to Jesus. The wide variation between the different explanations shows sufficiently how questionable the symbolic interpretation of the individual gifts is. It is inspired not by a solid exegesis but by ideas which are foreign to the text and which have been usually adopted for arbitrary reasons. The real meaning of the gifts is combined with the act of worship, 'and they fell down and worshipped him'. They constitute an act of homage to Jesus recognized as a king. More detailed interpretations go beyond the intention of the text.

Mt 2:1–12 reflects the contemporary experience of the early Christian community in the face of the negative reaction of Judaism as a whole to the message of Christ, although we should not overlook the many individual conversions stressed in the Acts of the Apostles. This rejection is *projected* by the evangelist into the very beginnings of the life and message of the Messiah. Still, in line with Israel's role as mediator, the Magi, representing the Gentiles, come to Jerusalem. It is only by means of the information which they receive there that they can find Jesus. Both Israel's vocation and the fact of its rejection of the Messiah are part of Matthew's picture. The homilist, therefore, cannot present this text as a wholesale condemnation of the Jews, represented here by Herod and the whole of Jerusalem (see the Second Vatican Council's *Constitution on the Jews*).

The manifestation or *epiphany* of Jesus, not the gifts, is the central point of the narrative and should be the core of the homily too.

The Magi, representing the Gentiles, come to Jerusalem, the goal of the Gentile pilgrimage (Isa 2:2–3; cf. Mt 8:11–12). The city reacts with fear, and as soon as the 'King of the Jews' is mentioned we have a presentiment of Jesus' rejection and crucifixion. The theme of the story of the Magi is the 'epiphany' of Jesus which draws the Gentiles to him and manifests the failure of the chosen people. 'The kingdom of God will be taken away from you and given to a nation producing the fruits of it' (Mt 21:43, the end of the parable of the wicked tenants who cast the son out of the vineyard and killed him).

Though Herod and the Magi are primarily representative figures, the homilist, in an effort to make the message of this episode relevant to our time, could develop the subordinate theme of the individual's reaction to Christ and the message of the gospel. Still we need to bear in mind that the primary concern of Matthew is not with Herod and the Magi, but with the manifestation of Christ in our world. By their act of homage the Magi profess that Christ is the king of the whole world.

The flight into Egypt (Mt 2:13–15)

This pericope is read on the Feast of the Holy Innocents, together with the pericope of the massacre of the innocents, Mt 2:16–18, and on the Feast of the Holy Family A, together with the pericope of the return from Egypt, Mt 2:19–23. Since this text seems to play a subordinate role in Matthew as a preparation for the massacre of the innocents and especially the return from Egypt, the new Exodus, and since it is always read in combination with either of these two narratives, there is no need to deal separately with it. It is possible that Matthew intended to recall the migration of Jacob-Israel to Egypt. So Jesus, embodiment of the new Israel, also goes to Egypt.

The massacre of the innocents (Mt 2:16–18)

Together with the flight into Egypt (Mt 2:13–15), this pericope constitutes the gospel reading for the Feast of the Holy Innocents.

It is improbable that Matthew is here relating an historical massacre, although Herod would have been perfectly capable of such a crime. The narrative seems to have been composed as part of the Jesus–Moses parallel, and in view of and with the help of the quotation from Jeremiah. The homilist, therefore, should refrain from giving a colourful picture of the massacre, but rather try to disclose the real message of the passage.

As Messiah and as one who fulfils the prophecies, Jesus is certainly 'greater than' Moses. But Matthew wants to show also that Jesus as the messianic teacher and promulgator of the perfect, radical will of God, is 'like' Moses. Matthew composes his narrative in such a way and with such parallels to the life of Moses that his first-century readers would easily see Jesus as 'like' Moses. This is already clear, for example, by comparing Mt 2:13–18 and Ex 1, but it becomes even more obvious if we compare Mt 2:13–23 with the Moses legends which were very popular in the first century A.D. In these we find an almost perfect parallel between the stories of Moses and those of Jesus.

At the beginning of his gospel, therefore, Matthew describes Jesus as the embodiment and the new leader of the new people of God. The note of opposition and rejection, already found in the story of the Magi, and in the message of the angel in Mt 2:14, is also included.

The return from Egypt (Mt 2:19–23)

This pericope constitutes the gospel reading of the Feast of the Holy Family A, together with Mt 2:13–15.

Again the homilist should not present the pericopes of the flight into Egypt and the return from Egypt as the record of historical incidents which need to be reconstructed as completely as possible adding details which have nothing to do with the true intent of Matthew's text. In fact, it should be noted that only by such questionable historicization is it possible to relate this gospel reading to the theme of the Holy Family.

The flight seems to have been narrated mainly as part of the return (exodus) from Egypt. While Matthew tells us about the flight 'to' Egypt, he says that this was to fulfil the prophetic words: 'Out of Egypt have I called my son!' Apparently, therefore, Matthew expects his readers to concentrate on the return from Egypt. Just as, when Pharaoh died, Moses was told to return to Egypt, so now that Herod is dead, Joseph is told to bring Jesus back to Israel. Because one of Herod's sons is king in Judea, Joseph does not go there but to Nazareth in Galilee, and here again scripture is fulfilled (Mt 2:23).

The homilist could refer to Mt 4:12–16 where it is stated that it was God's will as expressed in the scriptures (Isa 8:23 – 9:2[1]) that Jesus would begin his public ministry in Galilee. Apparently Matthew wants to stress both that the Messiah was born in Bethlehem and that he started his public ministry in Galilee (Nazareth). Both were God's will as expressed in scripture (Mt 2:5, Bethlehem; Mt 2:23, Nazarene-Nazareth), and, therefore, cannot contradict each other.

The underlying theme is God guiding the itinerary of his Messiah and, consequently of the messianic people, the Church which is always a community on the way, a pilgrim Church.

The annunciation of the birth of John the Baptist (Lk 1:5–25)

This passage is read on the Vigil of the Feast of John the Baptist (Lk 1:5–17) and on the Ferial of December 19.

The homilist should definitely avoid interpreting the dumbness of Zechariah as a punishment for lack of faith. For an unprepared audience it is best to abstain from mentioning this particular feature in a sermon. For a better prepared audience he could explain how Zechariah's dumbness is a sign of confirmation.

What else could the homilist use from this passage? He could point to the fact that Elizabeth's barrenness is not unique in scripture. Elizabeth was barren like Sarah, Rebekah, the mother of Samson, and the mother of Samuel. Like Abraham and Sarah, she and her husband were advanced in years and in human terms would have had to remain childless. This is not historical reporting, as if it pleased God to let all these people grow old without children to give them a child in their old age! It is a literary device to express the idea that God specially intervened at decisive moments of the history of his people and that the child to be born in this way is a special 'gift of God'. Luke affirms that John the Baptist was a child of grace like Isaac, Samson, and Samuel.

But it should also be stressed that the angel tells Zechariah: 'your prayer has been heard'. Just as the birth of Samuel was God's answer to the insistent prayers of Hannah, so the birth of John the Baptist is his answer to Zechariah's and Elizabeth's prayer. God's intervention in history is definitely his initiative, but it is not without human co-operation. God incorporates human aspirations and efforts into that realization of his plan. Men have to assume their responsibility.

The homilist could also concentrate on the person and mission of John the Baptist, especially on the Vigil of the Feast of John the Baptist. John will be guided by the creative power of God's Spirit. His task will be to prepare the coming of the Lord by bringing about a general reconciliation (see especially verses 16–17). Reconciliation is the true conversion Luke will have the Baptist preach: Lk 3:4–14. As Lk 3:10–14 especially shows, conversion and reconciliation are impossible without justice.

The annunciation of the birth of Jesus (Lk 1:26–38)

This pericope is read on the Fourth Sunday of Advent B, the Ferial of December 20, and the Feasts of the Annunciation and the Immaculate Conception.

Very few homilists pay enough attention to what this text has to say about Mary. Instead of letting the text speak, they tend to give free play to fantasies. The resulting portrayal of Mary runs counter to the text of the gospel, which contains no reference to Mary's virtues, piety, etc. Contrary to Lk 1:13 where Zechariah is told: 'Your prayer is heard', Mary is told: 'you have found favour with God' (Lk 1:30). It seems that Mary is chosen without any particular prayer on her part! Neither Mary nor the faithful profit from making her the subject of personal speculations that run counter to the text of scripture. Nobody can give Mary a more appropriate place than that given to her by scripture itself.

Homilists indulge in historical reconstructions of the annunciation story because they neglect to consider its literary form. Its structure has been determined not so much by any historical information Luke might have possessed, as by the patterns of *annunciation* and *call* narratives, both frequently found in the Old Testament.

The virginal conception of Jesus is undeniably one of the affirmations of the text but how it came about remains a mystery. The text does not contain the slightest indication of any attempt to give a physiological explanation of how the Spirit realized the conception of Jesus in Mary. The gospel is not interested in describing a biological process. Rather it proclaims that *Jesus has his origin in God*. With Jesus God initiated a *new beginning* by the power of the Holy Spirit.

Quite often Mary's question in Lk 1:34, 'How can this be, since I have no husband?' is understood as an expression of her vow of virginity, but such an explanation distorts the real purpose of this verse. It has a literary function in the structure of the pericope as a whole, namely the 'objection' on the part of the one called to a mission by God. Such an 'objection' does not imply any lack of faith in God, but expresses the limitations of the person called. Therefore, the refutation of the objection usually takes the form of a promise of assistance, e.g., 'I will be with you' (Judg 6:16), or 'The Holy Spirit will come upon you' (Lk 1:35). Thus the story suggests that, whatever a person may be called upon to do, in the final analysis it is God himself who acts through him or her. In the present text the message announces God's salvific initiative in and through Mary.

Christ is the focal point of the infancy narrative as a whole and of each and every pericope in particular. This should be taken into account while preaching the annunciation story. The correct understanding of the episode, therefore, does not permit a primarily Mariological interpretation. Mary's role is definitely subordinate. The story deals with the fulfilment of God's promises in Jesus. Any attempt to confine the scope of the annunciation to a private incident in Mary's life overlooks its universal saving dimension. If the homilist wants to preach on the role of Mary in this saving historical perspective, he will stress *God's choice* of Mary, not *Mary's merits*. It is to God and not to her husband or to her virginity that Mary owes Jesus. In Jesus God fulfils his promises; in Jesus the new creation begins. And Mary is God's instrument in bringing this about.

Who is Mary in the plan of God? The angel addresses Mary in the same words with which God addressed the *daughter of Zion* in Zephaniah. To Luke, Mary is this daughter of Zion of the endtime, the people of God, purified by God's love, where God can be completely at home. In Mary, God can come and live with his people. She is the figure of the Church of the endtime in which all of us will be found.

This is indicated by the new name given to Mary, 'full of grace'. This has been frequently interpreted in homilies as referring to Mary's virtues which made her the worthy recipient of this grace. But this is not the real meaning. When God gives somebody a new name, he does so to indicate what this person will be. God calls the trembling Gideon 'mighty man of valour', not because he is one, but because God is going to make him one (Judg 6:12). In her mission, Mary becomes 'full of grace'. Because of the connotations of this phrase, modern translators have preferred a better translation, 'favoured one' or 'highly favoured'. This same word is found only once elsewhere in the New Testament, where as a verb it refers to the Church of the endtime which God favours with grace in Jesus Christ (Eph 1:6). Mary prefigures what the transfigured Church will one day be.

The visitation and the Magnificat (Lk 1:39–56)

This pericope or part of it is read on several different days, the Ferial of December 21 (Lk 1:39–45), the Fourth Sunday of Advent C (Lk 1:39–45), the Solemnity of the Assumption of Mary (Lk 1:39–56), the Visitation (Lk 1:39–56), and the Ferial of December 22 (Lk 1:46–56).

The present text consists of a narrative introduction (Lk 1:39–45) and the *Magnificat* (Lk 1:46–55). The climax of the narrative is in the words: 'And blessed is she who believed that there would be a fulfilment of what was spoken to her from the Lord' (Lk 1:45). It stresses Mary's faith in response to God's initiative. Elizabeth's words, 'Blessed are you among women', do not refer to Mary's immaculate conception. Very similar words were addressed to Judith (Jud 13: 18–19). The narrative of the visitation is reminiscent of the transfer of the Ark of the Covenant to Jerusalem (cf. II Sam 6:2–11). Elizabeth's exclamation, 'Why is this granted me, that the mother of my Lord (= Messiah) should come to me?' recalls David's words, 'How can the Ark of the Lord (= God) come to me?' (II Sam 6:9).

Mary's faith in answer to God's initiative makes her the true dwelling-place of God among men. Luke has shown her to be such by comparing her to the Ark of the Covenant or to Zion itself. After the example of Mary, the Church, every Christian, is a sign of God's presence in the world: the attitudes and involvements of each Christian build the divine dwelling-place on earth.

The *Magnificat*, a mosaic of Old Testament texts attributed to Mary, does not enable us to describe the actual feelings of Mary, but rather to know what Luke and the early Church had to tell us about her. It is a hymn of praise in which Mary is presented as a person who thanks God for the wonderful things he has done in her and who places herself entirely at his disposal. In Mary's election and blessing, God came to his people's assistance. This is expressed in the last verse of the hymn: 'in remembrance of his mercy, as he spoke to our fathers, to Abraham and to his posterity for ever'. The saving history of Israel begins with Abraham's act of faith in response to God's initiative; the saving history of the new people of God, the Church, begins with Mary's act of faith in response to God's new intervention.

The birth and circumcision of John the Baptist (Lk 1:57–80)

Parts of this section of the infancy narrative are read on the Ferials of December 23 (Lk 1:57–66) and December 24 (Lk 1:67–79) and on the Feast of John the Baptist (Lk 1:57–66, 80).

The section has two major divisions: the narrative (Lk 1:57–66) and the *Benedictus* (Lk 1:67–79) to which the narrative forms the introduction. The conclusion (Lk 1:80) ties the incident to the wider story of John the Baptist (Lk 3:1–20). The birth of John marks the fulfilment of the angel's message to Zechariah and brings rejoicing; the completion of Elizabeth's term of pregnancy suggests the fulfilment of the messianic times. Luke narrates the circumcision because it was the occasion for the *name-giving*. John stands for *Johanan* or *Jehohanan* which means 'God's gracious gift'. All this serves as a narrative introduction to the *Benedictus* hymn.

The *Benedictus*, like the *Magnificat*, is a chain of Old Testament quotations and reminiscences, attributed by Luke to Zechariah. The literary structure of the canticle is centred on the parallelism of the 'Covenant' and the 'Oath' sworn to Abraham (verses 72–73). The whole of the canticle develops three themes: (1) God's benevolent intervention; (2) the salvation of the people; (3) the word of God.

The first part of the hymn praises God for his intervention in human history and its results. The second part describes the place that John the Baptist occupies in this mighty act of God. The central message of Zechariah's song is the same as Mary's: the great day for God's people in the coming of Jesus. John the Baptist's whole life was determined by his mission, for the Messiah and his people filled his life. God has chosen John to serve them.

The birth of Jesus (Lk 2:1–20)

Parts of this narrative are read during the Midnight Mass (Lk 2:1–14) and the Dawn Mass (Lk 2:15–20) of Christmas, and also on the Solemnity of Mary, Mother of God, January 1 (Lk 2:16–21). It is clear that Lk 2:1–20 and especially Lk 2:8–20 form an indivisible whole, and therefore it is unfortunate that the Lectionary cuts this section right in the middle! A better arrangement would be Lk 2:1–20 for the Midnight Mass and Lk 2:8–20 for the Mass at Dawn.

Although in scripture the birth of Jesus is of only secondary importance in comparison with his death and resurrection, many homilists accord it the first place. Often, thinking to put their hearers in a Christmas atmosphere, they base their considerations on legends which have nothing to do with the gospel text, reconstructing what they think must have been the historical circumstances of the birth of Jesus. In short, they aim to produce the same effect as the Nativity plays and Christmas cribs. This practice has to a large extent been responsible for the blurring of the true Christmas spirit. If we want to recover that spirit today we should first of all return to the simplicity and the soberness of the original text and to a correct, biblical interpretation of it.

The first part of the text focuses on the words: 'And she gave birth to her first-born son and wrapped him in swaddling cloths, and laid him in a manger, because there was no place for them in the inn' (Lk 2:7). It is, therefore, beside the point to refer to the swaddling cloths and the manger as indications that Jesus was born in poverty. If the homilist wants to preach about the poverty in which Jesus was born, this should not be done on the basis of the manger and the swaddling cloths, which say nothing to that effect. The only clear reference to the poverty in which Jesus was born is found in his presentation in the Temple, where we are told that Mary offered a pair of turtledoves (Lk 2:24), which Lev 12:8 tells us was the 'offering of the poor'. The statement, 'there was no place for them in the inn', is a sign neither of the alleged cruelty of the innkeeper nor of Mary's desire for privacy!

Luke does not tell us *how* Jesus was born, but rather suggests the *meaning* of this birth. The thrice-repeated 'manger' is the most important element. It is the place where the child is to be found. It is the symbol of God's being the sustenance of his people, a sustenance which people no longer knew how to find (Isa 1:3).

God gives them a sign, i.e., something that refers to something else. This sign is: you will find a baby in a manger. Note that the finding is part of the sign! The finding of the child in the manger is a sign that God wants to be found by his people again, to be recognized once more as his people's sustenance. God makes this possible in the child who is born, who should not stay in an 'inn', the place for a stranger (Jer 14:8), but rather in a manger, as God-with-us. The 'swaddling cloths' suggest a royal child, a son of David (Wis 7:3–4), fulfilling the promises of the Old Testament (e.g., II Sam 7:11–14; Isa 7:14).

Most homilists have the tendency to *canonize* the 'shepherds'. They are presented as devout people all the time looking forward to the coming of the Messiah while tending their flocks. In reality, contemporary Jewish literature considered them anything but a respectable class of people. They are repeatedly mentioned with tax-collectors and whores! But this is exactly Luke's point. If the shepherds are the first beneficiaries of this salvific event, it is not because they are deserving, devout people. They are outcasts, the last who become the first. Their election is a pure gift of grace. The Saviour of the poor and of sinners has been born. This interpretation is perfectly in keeping with the rest of Luke's gospel.

The 'glory' of the Lord has little to do with special light effects! The biblical idea of glory is first of all 'presence', God's presence revealed and experienced. In this particular case God's presence is revealed and experienced in the infant Jesus. However, we are not just celebrating the birthday of 'baby Jesus', but rather the dawn of the messianic salvation, of God's peace and favour towards mankind.

The 'peace' mentioned has nothing to do with 'peace of mind', but means rather that 'salvation' has now come upon the earth. Jesus is our peace (salvation) in his own person.

'Men of good will' is a Semitic expression which means men who are the object of *God's* good will or favour. This is why most translations prefer 'men with whom he is pleased'. This new translation should help correct the loose talk about 'men of good will' that usually goes on at Christmas time.

The naming and manifestation of Jesus (Lk 2:21–40)

This pericope or part of it is read on the Feast of the Holy Family B (Lk 2:22–40), the Feast of the Lord's Presentation (Lk 2:22–40), and the Ferials of December 29 (Lk 2:22–35) and 30 (Lk 2:36–40).

The circumcision and naming of Jesus and the Temple ritual introduce the main episode, the inspired witness of Simeon and Anna. To be named by God before birth was of great significance. For Luke as well as Matthew, it pointed to the nature of Jesus' destiny. The name Jesus means 'Yahweh saves'. The early Church apparently understood Jesus' presentation in the Temple as the fulfilment of the oracle of the prophet Malachi, 'the Lord whom you seek will suddenly come to his temple' (Mal 3:1).

The main idea is certainly that of the *manifestation* of Jesus. The testimony of Simeon stresses the *universality* of salvation in Jesus who is the 'salvation which God has prepared in the presence of all peoples, a light for revelation to the Gentiles, and for glory to your people Israel' (Lk 2:30–32). The homilist could develop the second part of the

Nunc Dimittis into a homily on Christ as the sign of contradiction and conflict then and now, starting from the words, 'this child is set for the fall and rising of many in Israel, and for a sign that is spoken against' (Lk 2:34).

In his final words Simeon tells Mary that the presentation of Jesus is the beginning of his sacrifice and hers. The sword that will pierce through Mary's soul is usually interpreted as a prophecy of her suffering at the foot of the cross. This is correct, but the meaning of the phrase should not be limited so narrowly. Rather, it is a sword whose thrust the whole of Israel will feel in the life and preaching of Christ, the sword of judgment. For Mary too, even before Calvary, there will be pain as she gradually gives up Jesus for his mission, the sword symbolizing separation. The following incident (Lk 2:41–52) is a first experience of this suffering which will reach its climax at the cross.

Jesus in the Temple (Lk 2:41–52)

This passage is read on the Feast of the Holy Family C, and on the Feast of St Joseph (Lk 2:41–51).

Many homilists have deprived this narrative of its true meaning on the level of salvation history, turning it into a piece of private family history. Instead of a self-revelation of the Messiah it becomes a story about a model child and a model family. The episode in Luke is rather a pronouncement story which finds its climax in Jesus' pronouncement: 'How is it that you sought me? Did you not know that I must be in my Father's house?' or (Jerusalem Bible) 'Did you not know that I must be busy with my Father's affairs?' (Lk 2:49).

The Church has taught from the earliest times that Jesus stands in a unique relationship to God. To the post-Easter faith, shared by Luke and his readers, Jesus appears as one who is so near to the Father that no human individual can have control over him. He must be where the Father is. The 'must' (Greek *dei*) mentioned here has the same meaning as in Lk 24:26, 'Was it not necessary (*dei*) that the Christ should suffer these things and enter into his glory?' It refers to the necessity which governs Jesus' messianic mission from beginning to end. Jesus here is not just giving children an example of obedience to parents!

It should also be noted that Jesus does not appear as a child wonder who is immediately recognizable as the Son of God. He listens and asks questions but all suggestions of a miraculous event are absent in the text. Luke says, however, that people 'were amazed at his understanding and his answers'. This may be alluding to the Book of Wisdom (Wis 8:10), and may thus be a comparison of Jesus with Solomon, the son of David. Later, this same gospel will quote Jesus as saying, 'for she (the queen of the South) came from the ends of the earth to hear the wisdom of Solomon, and behold, something greater than Solomon is here' (Lk 11:31).

To make this episode more concrete, the homilist may, for example, start from two features of the story, the fact that the parents mistakenly supposed that Jesus was with them (verses 43–44) and that 'they did not understand the saying which he spoke to them' (Lk 2:50). How often do we take it for granted that 'God is with us', that Christ is on our side, that our plans are his, to find out after some time that this is not really so, that our standards are not necessarily his. And so often we too do not understand the word Christ speaks to us. Each time we find ourselves mistaken we are invited to deepen our faith in the mystery of him who alone can reveal to us who he really is.

Notes

1. R. E. Brown, *The Virginal Conception and Bodily Resurrecton of Jesus* (New York/Paramus/Toronto: Paulist Press, 1973/London: Geoffrey Chapman, 1974), pp. 53–4.
2. A. G. Wright, *The Literary Genre Midrash* (Staten Island: Alba House, 1967), p. 74.
3. R. Le Déaut, 'Apropos a Definition of Midrash', *Interpretation* 25 (1971), 268–9.
4. R. Le Déaut, *ibid.*, 274–6.
5. Each of these passages begins with a genitive absolute construction. This is not found at the beginning of the massacre of the innocents (see Mt 2:16).
6. The Targums are records of oral Aramaic translations of the law and the prophets made during the public reading in the synagogues.
7. *Sefer ha-Zikhronoth*, found in pseudo-Philo, *Liber antiquitatum biblicarum*, a first-century work preserved only in Latin translation. It contains a series of legendary tales that expand the biblical data for the reader's edification.
8. M. J. Lagrange, *Évangile selon saint Matthieu* (Paris: Gabalda, 1932), p. 40 (quotation translated from the French).
9. G. M. Soares Prabhu, *The Formula Quotations in the Infancy Narrative of Matthew* (Analecta Biblica 63; Rome: Biblical Institute Press, 1976), p. 299.
10. In both Hebrew and Greek, the letters of the alphabet are also used as numerals; thus $d + w + d = 4 + 6 + 4 = 14$.
11. G. M. Soares Prabhu, *The Formula Quotations*, p. 243.
12. G. M. Soares Prabhu, *ibid.*, p. 232.
13. R. E. Brown, *The Birth of the Messiah. A Commentary on the Infancy Narratives in Matthew and Luke* (Garden City, N.Y.: Doubleday & Company, Inc./London: Geoffrey Chapman, 1977), pp. 135, 138–40.
14. R. E. Brown, *The Virginal Conception*, pp. 31–2.
15. R. E. Brown, *ibid.*, p. 66.
16. Cf. G. M. Soares Prabhu, *The Formula Quotations*, p. 267.
17. G. M. Soares Prabhu, *ibid.*, p. 281.
18. R. E. Brown, *The Birth of the Messiah*, pp. 181–3.
19. R. E. Brown, *ibid.*, p. 268.
20. L. Legrand, *L'Annonce à Marie (Lc 1, 26–38). Une apocalypse aux origines de l'Évangile* (Lectio Divina 106; Paris: Éditions du Cerf, 1981), pp. 67–87.

21. L. Legrand, *ibid.*, pp. 134–40.
22. R. E. Brown, *The Birth of the Messiah*, p. 312.
23. R. E. Brown, *ibid.*, pp. 363–4.
24. Rahab here is a mythical monster. There is no reference to Rahab of Jericho (Josh 2); the two words are spelt differently in Hebrew.
25. R. E. Brown, *An Adult Christ at Christmas* (Collegeville, Minn.: The Liturgical Press, 1977), p. 18.
26. R. E. Brown, *ibid.*, p. 19.
27. R. E. Brown, *The Birth of the Messiah*, p. 244.
28. R. E. Brown, *ibid.*, p. 483.

For Further Reading

Bligh, J., *The Infancy Narratives* (London: St Paul Publications, 1968).

Brown, R. E., *The Virginal Conception and Bodily Resurrection of Jesus* (New York/Paramus/Toronto: Paulist Press, 1973/London: Geoffrey Chapman, 1974).

Brown, R. E., *The Birth of the Messiah. A Commentary on the Infancy Narratives in Matthew and Luke* (Garden City, N.Y.: Doubleday & Company, Inc./London: Geoffrey Chapman, 1977).

Brown, R. E., *An Adult Christ at Christmas* (Collegeville, Minn.: The Liturgical Press, 1980).

Brown, R. E., *et al., Mary in the New Testament* (Philadelphia: Fortress Press/New York: Paulist Press, 1978/London: Geoffrey Chapman, 1979).

Dalton, W., *Mary in the New Testament* (Melbourne: Spectrum Publications, 1974).

Daniélou, J., *The Infancy Narratives* (New York: Herder and Herder/London: Burns and Oates, 1968).

Dodd, C. H., *The Founder of Christianity* (New York: The Macmillan Co., 1970/London: Collins, 1971).

Hermans, L., *The Bible on the Childhood of Jesus* (De Pere, Wisc.: St Norbert Abbey Press/London: Sheed and Ward, 1965).

Kamphaus, F., *The Gospels for Preachers and Teachers* (London: Sheed and Ward, 1974).

Richards, H. J., *The First Christmas. What Really Happened?* (Fontana Books; London: Collins, 1973).

General Bibliography

Abel, E. L., 'The Geneaologies of Jesus O XPICTOC', *New Testament Studies* 20 (1973–74), 203–10.

Aschbeck, D., 'The Literary Genre of Matthew 1 – 2', *The Bible Today* no. 57 (December 1971), 572–8.

Audet, J. P., 'L'Annonce à Marie', *Revue Biblique* 63 (1956), 346–74.

Auffret, P., 'Note sur la Structure littéraire de Lc. I, 68–79', *New Testament Studies* 24 (1977–78), 248–58.

Baarda, T., ' "Nunc Dimittis . . ." ' Annotaties bij Lukas 2:29–30' in *Zending op weg naar de toekomst. Essays aangeboden aan Prof. Dr. J. Verkuyl* (Kampen: Kok, 1978), pp. 59–79.

Bailey, K. E., 'The Song of Mary: Vision of a New Exodus (Luke 1:46–55)', *Near East School of Theology Theological Review* 2 (1979), 29–35.

Bailey, K. E., 'The Manger and the Inn: The Cultural Background of Luke 2:7', *ibid.*, 35–44.

Baily, M., 'The Crib and Exegesis of Luke 2:1–20', *Irish Ecclesiastical Record* 100 (1963), 359–76.

Baily, M., 'The Shepherds and the Sign of a Child in a Manger', *Irish Theological Quarterly* 31 (1964), 1–23.

Barclay, W., *The First Three Gospels* (London: SCM Press/Philadelphia: Westminster Press, 1966).

Beck, E., *Gottes Sohn kam in die Welt. Sachbuch zu den Weihnachtstexten* (Stuttgart: Verlag Katholisches Bibelwerk, 1978).

Beckwith, R. T., 'St Luke, the Date of Christmas and the Priestly Courses at Qumran', *Revue de Qumran* 9 (1977), 73–94.

Benko, S., 'The Magnificat. A History of Controversy', *Journal of Biblical Literature* 86 (1967), 263–76.

Benoit, P., 'L'enfance de Jean-Baptiste selon Luc 1', *New Testament Studies* 3 (1956–57), 169–94.

Benoit, P., ' "Et toi-même, un glaive te transpercera l'âme" (Luc 2, 35)', *The Catholic Biblical Quarterly* 25 (1963), 251–61.

Bergant, D., 'Bethlehem – Ephrathah', *The Bible Today* 20 (no. 1, January 1982), 26–7.

Bertram, R. W., 'An Epiphany Crossing – Programming Matthew 2:1–12 for Readers Today', *Currents in Theology and Mission* 7 (1980), 328–36.

Beverly, H., 'Lk 1:39–45', *Interpretation* 30 (1976), 396–404.

Bloch, R., ' "Juda engendra Pharès et Zara, de Thamar" (Matth 1:3)' in *Mélanges Bibliques rédigés en l'honneur d'André Robert* (Paris: Bloud & Gay, 1955), pp. 381–9.

Bostock, D. G., 'Jesus as the New Elijah', *Expository Times* 92 (2, 1980), 39–41.

Bourke, M. M., 'The Literary Genus of Matthew 1 – 2', *The Catholic Biblical Quarterly* 22 (1960), 160–75.

Bouton, A.,' "C'est toi qui donnera le nom de Jésus" Mt 1:18–24', *Assemblées du Seigneur* 8 (1973), 17–25.

Brennan, J. P., 'Virgin and Child in Isaiah 7:14', *The Bible Today* no. 15 (December 1964), 968–74.

Brock, S., 'Passover, Annunciation and Epiclesis: Some Remarks on the Term *aggen* in the Syriac Versions of Lk 1:35', *Novum Testamentum* 24 (1982), 222–33.

Brown, R. E., 'Luke's Description of the Virginal Conception', *Theological Studies* 35 (1974), 360–2.

Brown, R. E., 'The Meaning of the Magi; The Significance of the Star', *Worship* 49 (1975), 574–82.

Brown, R. E., 'The Meaning of the Manger; The Significance of the Shepherds', *Worship* 50 (1976), 528–38.

Brown, R. E., 'The Presentation of Jesus (Luke 2:22–40)', *Worship* 51 (1977), 2–11.

Brown, R. E., 'The Finding of the Boy Jesus in the Temple; A Third Christmas Story', *ibid.*, 474–85. (This and the three preceding articles are also collected in *An Adult Christ at Christmas*: see *For Further Reading* above.)

Brown, R. E., 'Luke's Method in the Annunciation Narratives of Chapter One' in *Perspectives on Luke-Acts* (ed. C. H. Talbert; Danville, Va.: Association of Baptist Professors of Religion, 1978/Edinburgh: T. & T. Clark, 1979), pp. 126–38.

Brown, R. E., 'Rachab in Mt 1, 5 Probably is Rahab of Jericho', *Biblica* 63 (1982), 79–80.

Bruns, J. E., 'The Magi Episode in Matthew 2', *The Catholic Biblical Quarterly* 22 (1961), 51–4.

Bruns, J. E., 'Matthew's Genealogy of Jesus', *The Bible Today* no. 15 (December 1964), 980–5.

Buby, B., 'The Biblical Prayer of Mary (Luke 2:19, 51)', *Review for Religious* 39 (1980), 577–81.

Bulbeck, R., 'The Doubt of St Joseph', *The Catholic Biblical Quarterly* 10 (1948), 296–309.

Byrne, M., 'No Room for the Inn', *Search* 5 (1982), 37–40.

Cambe, M., 'La *charis* chez saint Luc. Remarques sur quelques texts, notamment le *kecharitōmenē*', *Revue Biblique* 70 (1963), 193–207.

Cantwell, L., 'The Parentage of Jesus: Mt I, 18–21', *Novum Testamentum* 24 (1982), 304–15.

Carmignac, J., 'The Meaning of *Parthenos* in Luke 1.27. A Reply to C. H. Dodd', *The Bible Translator* 28 (1977), 327–30.

Cave, C. H., 'St Matthew's Infancy Narrative', *New Testament Studies* 9 (1962–63), 382–90.

Charlier, J.-P., 'Du berceau au tombeau. Préface et postface de l'évangile de Matthieu', *Vie Spirituelle* 133 (no. 630, 1979), 8–25; (no. 631, 1979), 172–91.

Couroyer, B., 'A propos de Luc II, 52', *Revue Biblique* 86 (1979), 92–101.

Cousin, H., 'Une autre exégèse de la conception virginale est-elle possible?', *Lumière et Vie* 23 (no. 119, 1974), 106–11.

da Spinetoli, O., 'Les généalogies de Jésus et leur signification. Mt 1, 1–25; Lc 3, 23–38', *Assemblées du Seigneur* 9 (1974), 6–19.

Davis, C. T., 'Tradition and Redaction in Matthew 1:18 – 2:23', *Journal of Biblical Literature* 90 (1971), 404–21.

Davis, C. T., 'The Fulfillment of Creation: A Study of Matthew's Genealogy', *Journal of the American Academy of Religion* 41 (1973), 520–35.

Delling, G., '*magos, mageia, mageuō*' in *Theological Dictionary of the New Testament* IV (ed. G. Kittel; Grand Rapids: Eerdmans/London, SCM Press, 1967), pp. 356–9.

Denis, A. M., 'L'adoration des Mages vue par S. Matthieu', *Nouvelle Revue Théologique* 82 (1960), 32–9.

Derrett, J. D. M., 'The Manger: Ritual Law and Soteriology', *Theology* 74 (no. 618, 1971), 566–71.

Derrett, J. D. M., 'Further Light on the Narratives of the Nativity', *Novum Testamentum* 17 (1975), 81–108.

Dignath, W., *Die lukanische Vorgeschichte* (Handbücherei für den Religionsunterricht 8; Gütersloh: Verlagshaus Gerd Mohn, 1971).

Dodd, C. H., *According to the Scriptures* (Fontana Books; London: Collins, 1965).

Dodd, C. H., 'New Testament Translation Problems II', *The Bible Translator* 28 (1977), 101–16.

Down, M. J., 'The Matthean Birth Narratives: Matthew 1:18 – 2:23', *Expository Times* 90 (1978–79), 51–2.

Dubarle, A. M., 'La conception virginale et la citation d'Is., VII, 14 dans l'Évangile de Matthieu', *Revue Biblique* 85 (1978), 362–80.

Dupont, J., 'Luc 2, 41–52. Jésus à douze ans', *Assemblées du Seigneur* 14 (1961), 25–43.

Dupont, J., 'Le Magnificat comme discours sur Dieu', *Nouvelle Revue Théologique* 102 (1980), 321–43.

Dupont, J., 'The Magnificat as God-talk', *Theology Digest* 29 (1981), 153–4.

Evans, C. F., 'Tertullian's References to Sentius Saturninus and the Lukan Census', *Journal of Theological Studies* 24 (1973), 24–39.

Farris, S. C., 'On Discerning Semitic Sources in Luke 1 – 2' in *Gospel Perspectives. Studies of History and Tradition in the Four Gospels* (ed. R. T. France and D. Wenham; Sheffield: JSOT Press, 1980–81), Vol. II, pp. 201–37.

Félicé, A., ' "Hoe zal dit geschieden?" (Luc 1, 34). Geen onverenigbare uitspraken in de H. Schrift omtrent Maria's maagdelijk moederschap', *Emmaüs* 10 (1979), 76–89.

Fenton, J. C., 'Matthew and the Divinity of Jesus: Three Questions concerning Matthew 1:20–23' in *Studia Biblica 1978*, II: *Papers on the Gospels* (ed. E. A. Livingstone; Sheffield: JSOT Press, 1980). pp. 79–82.

Feuillet, A., *Jésus et sa Mère d'après les récits lucaniens de l'enfance et d'après Saint Jean* (Paris: Gabalda, 1973).

Figueras, P., 'Syméon et Anne, ou le témoignage de la loi et des prophètes', *Novum Testamentum* 20 (1978), 84–99.

Fitzmyer, J. A., ' "Peace on Earth among Men of His Good Will" (Lk 2:14)', *Theological Studies* 19 (1958), 225–7.

Fitzmyer, J. A., 'The Virginal Conception of Jesus in the New Testament', *Theological Studies* 34 (1973), 541–75.

Ford, J. M., 'Zealotism and the Lukan Infancy Narratives', *Novum Testamentum* 18 (1976), 280–92.

France, R. T., 'Herod and the Children of Bethlehem', *Novum Testamentum* 21 (1979), 98–120.

France, R. T., 'The "Massacre of the Innocents" – Fact or Fiction?' in *Studia Biblica 1978*, II: *Papers on the Gospels* (ed. E. A. Livingstone; Sheffield: JSOT Press, 1980), pp. 83–94.

France, R. T., 'The Formula Quotations of Matthew 2 and the Problem of Communication', *New Testament Studies* 27 (1980–81), 233–51.

Gaechter, P., 'Die Magierperikope (Mt 2, 1–12)', *Zeitschrift für Katholische Theologie* 90 (1968), 257–95.

Gaston, L., 'The Lukan Birth Narratives in Tradition and Redaction' in *Society of Biblical Literature 1976 Seminar Papers* (ed. G. McRae; Missoula, Mont.: Scholars Press, 1976), pp. 209–18.

George, A., 'Le parallèle entre Jean-Baptiste et Jésus en Lc 1 – 2' in *Mélanges Bibliques en hommage au R. P. Béda Rigaux* (ed. A. Descamps and A. de Halleux; Gembloux: Duculot, 1970), pp. 147–71.

Gibbs, J. M., 'Purpose and Pattern in Matthew's Use of the Title "Son of David"', *New Testament Studies* 10 (1963–64), 446–64; especially 447–8.

Giblin, C. H., 'Reflections on the Sign of the Manger', *The Catholic Biblical Quarterly* 29 (1967), 87–101.

Globe, A., 'Some Doctrinal Variants in Matthew 1 and Luke 2 and the Authority of the Neutral Text', *The Catholic Biblical Quarterly* 42 (1980), 52–72.

Gordon, C. H., 'Paternity at Two Levels', *Journal of Biblical Literature* 96 (1977), 101.

Gordon, C. H., 'The Double Paternity of Jesus', *Biblical Archaeology Review* 4 (1978), 26–7.

Grelot, P., 'La naissance d'Isaac et celle de Jésus', *Nouvelle Revue Théologique* 94 (1972), 462–87.

Gryglewicz, F., 'Die Herkunft der Hymnen des Kindheitsevangelium des Lucas', *New Testament Studies* 21 (1974–75), 265–73.

Gueuret, A., 'Luc I – II. Analyse Sémiotique', *Sémiotique et Bible* 25 (1982), 35–42.

Gueuret, A., *L'engendrement d'un récit: L'évangile de l'enfance selon saint Luc* (Lectio Divina 113; Paris: Éditions du Cerf, 1983).

Gutbrod, K., *Die 'Weihnachtsgeschichten' des Neuen Testaments* (Stuttgart: Calwer Verlag, 1971).

Halpern, B., 'Ritual Background of Zechariah's Temple Song', *The Catholic Biblical Quarterly* 40 (1978), 167–80.

Hamel, F., 'Le Magnificat et le renversement des situations. Réflexion théologico-biblique', *Gregorianum* 60 (1979), 55–84.

Hammer, W., 'L'intention de la généalogie de Matthieu', *Études Théologiques et Religieuses* 55 (1980), 305–6.

Hanson, R. S., 'Mary, According to Luke', *Worship* 43 (1969), 425–9.

Hayles, D. J., 'The Roman Census and Jesus' Birth. Was Luke Correct? Part I: The Roman Census System', *Buried History* 9 (1973), 113–32.

Hayles, D. J., 'The Roman Census and Jesus' Birth. Was Luke Correct? Part

II: Quirinius' Career and a Census in Herod's Day', *Buried History* 10 (1974), 16–31.

Hengel, M., and Merkel, H., 'Die Magier aus dem Osten und die Flucht nach Ägypten (Mt 2) im Rahmen der antiken Religionsgeschichte und der Theologie des Matthäus' in *Orientierung an Jesus* (ed. P. Hoffmann; Freiburg: Herder, 1973), pp. 139–69.

Hofkens, J., 'Het kind op de katheder, ". . . te midden van de leraren luisterend en vragen stellend" (Lc 2, 46)', *Emmaüs* 10 (1979), 71–5.

Horst, P. W. van der, 'Notes on the Aramaic Background of Luke II. 41–52', *Journal for the Study of the New Testament* 7 (1980), 61–6.

Hospodar, B., '*Meta spoudēs* in Luke 1, 39', *The Catholic Biblical Quarterly* 18 (1956), 14–18.

Hunzinger, C. H., 'Neues Licht auf Lc 2:14 *anthrōpoi eudokias*', *Zeitschrift für die Neutestamentliche Wissenschaft* 44 (1952–53), 85–90.

Hunzinger, C. H., 'Ein weiterer Beleg zu Lc 2, 14', *Zeitschrift für die Neutestamentliche Wissenschaft* 49 (1958), 129–30.

Iersel, B. van, 'The Finding of Jesus in the Temple. Some Observations on the Original Form of Luke II. 41–51a', *Novum Testamentum* 4 (1960), 161–73.

Jacquemin, P.-E., 'Le Magnificat. Lc 1:46–55', *Assemblées du Seigneur* 66 (1973), 28–40.

Jansen, J., 'Luke 2:41–52', *Interpretation* 30 (1976), 400–4.

Jeremias, J., '*Anthrōpoi eudokias* (Lc 2:14)', *Zeitschrift für die Neutestamentliche Wissenschaft* 28 (1929), 13–20.

Jones, D., 'The Background and Character of the Lukan Psalms', *Journal of Theological Studies* 19 (1968), 19–50.

Jonge, H. J. de, 'Sonship, Wisdom, Infancy: Luke II. 41–51a', *New Testament Studies* 24 (1977–78), 317–54.

Kaiser, W. C., 'The Promise and the Arrival of Elijah in Malachi and the Gospels', *Grace Theological Journal* 3 (1982), 221–33.

Kevers, P., 'Hoe zal dit geschieden? Het boodschapsverhaal van Lucas in het licht van het Oud Testament', *Tijdschrift voor Geestelijk Leven* 33 (1977), 577–95.

King, P., 'Matthew and Epiphany', *Worship* 36 (1962), 89–94.

King, P., 'Elizabeth, Zachary, and the Messiah', *The Bible Today* no. 15 (December 1964), 992–7.

Klaiber, W., 'Eine lukanische Fassung des sola gratia. Beobachtungen zu Lk 1, 5–6' in *Rechtfertigung. Festschrift für Ernst Käsemann* (ed. J. Friedrich *et al.*; Tübingen: J. C. B. Mohr, 1976), pp. 211–18.

Knoerzer, W., *Wir haben seinen Stern gesehen. Die Kindheitsevangelien nach Lukas und Matthäus* (Stuttgart: Verlag Katholisches Bibelwerk, 1968).

Kraemer, M., 'Die Menschwerdung Jesu Christi nach Matthäus (Mt 1). Sein Anliegen und sein literarischen Verfahren', *Biblica* 45 (1964), 1–50.

Krentz, E., 'The Extent of Matthew's Prologue. Toward the Structure of the First Gospel', *Journal of Biblical Literature* 83 (1964), 409–14.

Lagrand, J., 'How was the Virgin Mary "Like a Man" . . . ? A Note on Mt I. 18b and Related Syriac Christian Texts', *Novum Testamentum* 22 (1980), 97–107.

Lambrecht, J., 'The Child in the Manger: A Meditation on Lk 2:1–20', *Louvain Studies* 5 (1974–75), 331–5.

General Bibliography 139

Laurentin, R., *Structure de Luc I – II* (Études Bibliques; Paris: J. Gabalda et Cie, Éditeurs, 1957).

Laurentin, R., 'Les Évangiles de l'enfance', *Lumière et Vie* 23 (no. 119, 1974), 84–105.

Laurentin, R., *Les évangiles de l'enfance du Christ: Vérité de Noël au-delà des mythes: Exégèse et sémiotique – historicité et théologie* (Paris: Desclée de Brouwer, 1982).

Lauverjat, M., 'Luc 2: une simple approche', *Sémiotique et Bible* 27 (1982), 31–47.

Leaney, A. R. C., 'The Birth Narratives of St Luke and St Matthew', *New Testament Studies* 8 (1961–62), 158–66.

Le Déaut, R., 'Apropos a Definition of Midrash', *Interpretation* 25 (1971), 259–82.

Legrand, L., *The Biblical Doctrine of Virginity* (London: Geoffrey Chapman/New York: Sheed and Ward, 1963).

Legrand, L., 'L'arrière-plan néotestamentaire de Lc. 1, 35', *Revue Biblique* 70 (1963), 161–92.

Legrand, L., 'L'Évangile aux Bergers. Essai sur le genre littéraire de Lc 2, 8–20', *Revue Biblique* 75 (1968), 161–87.

Legrand, L., *L'annonce à Marie (Lc 1, 26–38)* (Lectio Divina 106; Paris: Éditions du Cerf, 1981).

Legrand, L., ' "On l'appela du nom de Jésus" (Luc II, 21)', *Revue Biblique* 89 (1982), 481–91.

Léon-Dufour, X., 'Le Juste Joseph', *Nouvelle Revue Théologique* 81 (1959), 225–31.

Léon-Dufour, X., 'Libro della Genesi di Gesù Cristo', *Rivista Biblica* 13 (1965), 223–37.

Lerle, E., 'Die Ahnenverzeichnisse Jesu. Versuch einer christologischen Interpretation', *Zeitschrift für die Neutestamentliche Wissenschaft* 72 (1981), 112–17.

Linskens, J., 'Mary in the New Testament', *Contemporary Studies* 4 (1967), 96–105, 164–71.

Lüthi, W., 'Friede, ein anständiges Wort? Predigt über Lukas 2, 14', *Theologische Beiträge* 12 (1981), 249–53.

McGrath, B., 'He Came All So Still', *The Bible Today* no. 9 (December 1963), 580–5.

McHugh, J., 'A New Approach to the Infancy Narratives', *Marianum* 40 (1978), 277–87.

McNamara, M., 'Were the Magi Essenes?', *Irish Ecclesiastical Record* 110 (1968), 305–28.

Maillot, A., 'Quelques remarques sur la Naissance Virginale du Christ', *Foi et Vie* 77 (1978), 30–44.

Maier, P. L., 'The Infant Massacre – History or Myth?', *Christianity Today* 20 (1975), 299–302.

Malina, B., 'Matthew 2 and Isa 41, 2–3: a Possible Relationship?', *Studii Biblici Franciscani Liber Annuus* 17 (1967), 290–302.

Maly, E. H., 'Now it came to pass in those days . . .', *The Bible Today* no. 3 (December 1962), 173–8.

Manns, F., 'Luc 2, 41–50 témoin de la bar Mitswa de Jésus', *Marianum* 40 (1978), 344–9.

Martin, J. P., 'Luke 1:39–47', *Interpretation* 36 (1982), 394–9.

Masson, J., *Jésus Fils de David dans les généalogies de saint Matthieu et saint Luc* (Paris: Téqui, 1982).

Medisch, R., 'Ein neuer Kommentar zu den Kindheitsgeschichten', *Theologie der Gegenwart* 22 (1979), 242–7.

Mercurio, R., 'The Shepherds at the Crib. A Lukan Vignette', *The Bible Today* no. 3 (December 1962), 141–5.

Meyer, B. F., ' "But Mary Kept all these Things" (Lk 2, 19.51)', *The Catholic Biblical Quarterly* 26 (1964), 31–49.

Meyer, B. F., 'A Word of Simeon', *The Bible Today* no. 15 (December 1964), 998–1002.

Milavec, A., 'Matthew's Integration of Sexual and Divine Begetting', *Biblical Theology Bulletin* 8 (1978), 108–16.

Miller, C. H., 'Herod and His Family', *The Bible Today* no. 45 (December 1969), 3106–13.

Milton, H., 'The Structure of the Prologue of Matthew's Gospel', *Journal of Biblical Literature* 81 (1962), 175–81.

Minear, P., 'Luke's Use of the Birth Stories' in *Studies in Luke-Acts* (ed. L. E. Keck and J. L. Martyn; New York: Abingdon Press, 1966/London: SPCK, 1968), pp. 111–30.

Miranda, J. P., 'Empfängnis und Geburt Christi', *Texte und Kontexte* no. 8 (1980), 45–61.

Miyoshi, M., 'Jesu Darstellung oder Reinigung im Tempel under Berücksichtigung von "Nunc Dimittis" Lk II, 22–38', *Annual of the Japanese Biblical Institute* 4 (1978), 85–115.

Moloney, F. J., 'The Infancy Narratives. Another View of Raymond Brown's "The Birth of the Messiah"', *The Clergy Review* 64 (1979), 161–6.

Mount, W., 'Jesus in Luke 1 – 2. Some Aspects of Luke's Editorial Work', *Perkins School of Theology Journal* 26 (1972), 41–6.

Muñoz Iglesias, S., 'El Evangelio de la Infancia en S. Mateo' in *Sacra Pagina. Miscellanea Biblica Congressus Internationalis Catholici de Re Biblica* (ed. J. Coppens, A. Descamps and E. Massaux; Paris/Gembloux: Librairie Lecoffre /Éditions J. Duculot, 1959), Vol. II, pp. 121–49.

Muñoz Iglesias, S., 'Literary Genre of the Infancy Gospel', *Theology Digest* 9 (1961), 15–25.

Muñoz Iglesias, S., 'Midráš y Evangelios de la Infancia', *Estudios Eclesiásticos* 47 (1972), 331–50.

Muñoz Iglesias, S., 'La concepción virginal de Cristo en los Evangelios de la Infancia', *Estudios Bíblicos* 31 (1978), 5–28, 213–41.

Murphy, R. T. A., 'On Shepherds', *The Bible Today* no. 15 (December 1964), 986–91.

Murphy-O'Connor, J., 'Bookreview on G. M. Soares Prabhu, *The Formula Quotations in the Infancy Narrative of Matthew*', *Revue Biblique* 84 (1977), 292–7.

Neirynck, F., ' "Maria bewaarde al de woorden in haar hart." Lk 2, 19.51 in hun context verklaard', *Collationes Brugenses et Gandavenses* 5 (1959), 433–66.

Neirynck, F., 'Bijdrage tot de Quellenanalyse van Lk 1 – 2', *Collationes Brugenses et Gandavenses* 6 (1960), 387–404.

Neirynck, F., *L'Évangile de Noël* (Études Religieuses no. 749; Paris/Brussels: Office Général du Livre/La Pensée Catholique, 1960).

Nellessen, E., *Das Kind und seine Mutter. Struktur und Verkündigung des 2.*

Kapitels im Matthäusevangelium (Stuttgarter Bibelstudien 39; Stuttgart: Verlag Katholisches Bibelwerk, 1970).

Newman, B. M., Jr, 'Matthew 1.1–8: Some Comments and a Suggested Restructuring', *The Bible Translator* 27 (1976), 209–12.

Nineham, D. E., 'The Genealogy in St Matthew's Gospel and its Significance for the Study of the Gospels', *Bulletin of the John Rylands University Library, Manchester* 58 (1976), 421–44.

Nolan, B. M., *The Royal Son of God. The Christology of Matthew 1 – 2 in the Setting of the Gospel* (Orbis Biblicus et Orientalis 23; Fribourg, Switz.: Éditions Universitaires, 1979).

O'Fearghail, F., 'The Literary Form of Lk 1, 5–25 and 1, 26–38', *Marianum* 43 (3–4, 1981), 321–44.

Ogg, G., 'The Quirinius Question Today', *Expository Times* 79 (1967–68), 231–6.

Oliver, H. H., 'The Lucan Birth Stories and the Purpose of Luke-Acts', *New Testament Studies* 10 (1963–64), 202–26.

O'Neill, J. C., 'Glory to God in the Highest. And on Earth?' in *Biblical Studies* (ed. J. R. McKay; London: Collins/Philadelphia: Westminster Press, 1976), pp. 172–7.

Overstreet, R. L., 'Difficulties in New Testament Genealogies', *Grace Theological Journal* 2 (1981), 303–26.

Pascual, E., 'La Genealogía de Jesús según S. Mateo', *Estudios Bíblicos* 23 (1964), 109–49.

Paul, A., *L'évangile de l'enfance selon Matthieu* (Lire la Bible 17; Paris: Éditions du Cerf, 1968).

Perrot, C., 'Les récits d'enfance dans la Haggada antérieure au II siècle de notre ère', *Recherches de Science Religieuse* 55 (1967), 481–518.

Pesch, R., 'Der Gottessohn im matthäischen Evangeliumsprolog (Mt 1 – 2). Beobachtungen zu den Zitationsformeln der Reflexionszitate', *Biblica* 48 (1967), 395–420.

Pesch, R. (ed.), *Zur Theologie der Kindheitsgeschichten. Der heutige Stand der Exegese* (Schriftenreihe der katholischen Akademie der Erzdiözese Freiburg; Munich/Zürich: Verlag Schnell & Steiner, 1981).

Quinn, J. D., 'Mary, Seat of Wisdom', *The Bible Today* no. 12 (March 1964), 787–92.

Quinn, J. D., 'Is *Rachab* in Mt 1,5 Rahab of Jericho?', *Biblica* 62 (1981), 225–8.

Raatschen, J. H., 'Empfangen durch den Heiligen Geist. Überlegungen zu Mt 1, 18–25', *Theologische Beiträge* 11 (1980), 262–77.

Racette, J., 'L'évangile de l'enfance selon saint Matthieu', *Sciences Ecclésiastiques* 9 (1957), 77–85.

Ramaroson, L., 'Ad structuram cantici "Magnificat"', *Verbum Domini* 46 (1968), 30–46.

Ramlot, L., 'Les généalogies bibliques. Un genre littéraire oriental', *Bible et Vie Chrétienne* 60 (1964), 53–70.

Redford, J., 'The Quest of the Historical Epiphany. Critical Reflections on Raymond Brown's "The Birth of the Messiah"', *The Clergy Review* 64 (1979), 5–11.

Romaniuk, K., '"Joseph, son époux, qui était un homme juste ne voulait pas la dénoncer . . ." (Mt 1,19)', *Collectanea Theologica* 50 (special issue 1980), 123–31.

Rosa, G. de, 'Storia e teologia nei racconti dell'infanzia di Gesù', *Civiltà Cattolica* 129 (no. 3084, 1978), 521–37.

Rosenberg, R. A., 'The "Star of the Messiah" Reconsidered', *Biblica* 53 (1972), 105–9.

Ruddick, C. T., 'Birth Narratives in Genesis and Luke', *Novum Testamentum* 12 (1970), 343–48.

Ruger, H. P., '*Nazareth/Nazara. Nazarēnos/Nazaraios*', *Zeitschrift für die neutestamentliche Wissenschaft* 72 (1981), 257–63.

Sabourin, L., 'Recent Views on Luke's Infancy Narratives', *Religious Studies Bulletin* 1 (1981), 18–25.

Sabourin, L., 'Two Lukan Texts (1:35; 3:22)', *ibid.*, 29–33.

Schaeder, H., '*Nazarēnos, Nazōraios*' in *Theological Dictionary of the New Testament* IV (ed. G. Kittel; Grand Rapids: Eerdmans/London, SCM Press, 1967), pp. 847–79.

Schelkle, K. H., 'Die Frauen im Stammbaum Jesu', *Bibel und Kirche* 18 (1963), 113–15.

Schlüsser-Fiorenza, E., 'Luke 2:41–52', *Interpretation* 36 (1982), 399–403.

Schmahl, G., 'Lk 2, 41–52 und die Kindheitserzählung des Thomas 19, 1–5. Ein Vergleich', *Bibel und Leben* 15 (1974), 249–58.

Schmahl, G., 'Magier aus dem Osten und die Heiliger Drei Könige', *Trierer Theologische Zeitschrift* 87 (1978), 295–303.

Schmidt, P., 'Maria in der Sicht des Magnifikat', *Geist und Leben* 46 (1973), 417–30.

Schmidt, P., 'Maria und das Magnificat. Maria im Heilshandeln Gottes im Alten und Neuen Gottesvolk', *Catholica* 29 (1975), 230–46.

Schmithals, W., 'Die Weihnachtsgeschichte Lukas 2, 1–20' in *Festschrift für Ernst Fuchs* (ed. G. Ebeling, E. Jüngel and G. Schunack; Tübingen: Mohr, 1973), pp. 281–97.

Schnackenburg, R., 'Das Magnificat, seine Spiritualität und Theologie', *Geist und Leben* 38 (1965), 342–57.

Schneider, G., 'Lk 1, 34.35 als redaktionelle Einheit', *Biblische Zeitschrift* 15 (1971), 255–9.

Schnider, F., and Stenger, W., 'Die Frauen im Stammbaum Jesu nach Matthäus. Strukturale Beobachtungen zu Mt. 1, 1–17', *Biblische Zeitschrift* 23 (1979), 187–96.

Schnider, F., and Stenger, W.,' "Mit der Abstammung Jesu Christi verhielt es sich so." Strukturale Beobachtungen zu Mt 1, 18–25', *Biblische Zeitschrift* 25 (1981), 225–64.

Schoenberg, M. W., 'The Theological Significance of Bethlehem', *The Bible Today* no. 3 (December 1962), 153–7.

Schottroff, L., 'Das Magnificat und die älteste Tradition über Jesus von Nazareth', *Evangelische Theologie* 38 (1978), 298–313.

Schrage, W., 'Was fallt dem Exegeten zu Weihnachten ein?', *Der Evangelische Erzieher* 31 (1979), 338–44.

Schubert, K., 'Die Kindheitgeschichten Jesu im Lichte der Religionsgeschichte des Judentums', *Bibel und Liturgie* 45 (1972), 224–40.

Schürmann, H., 'Aufbau, Eigenart und Geschichtswert der Vorgeschichte Lk 1 – 2' in *Traditionsgeschichtliche Untersuchungen zu den synoptischen Evangelien* (Düsseldorf: Patmos, 1968), pp. 198–208.

Schweizer, E., ' "Er wird Nazoräer heissen" (zu Mc 1, 24; Mt 2, 23)' in

Judentum – Urchristentum – Kirche. Festschrift für J. Jeremias (ed. W. Eltester; Berlin: Verlag A. Töpelmann, 1960), pp. 90–3.

Schweizer, E., *Neues Testament und Christologie im Werden. Aufsätze* (Göttingen: Vandenhoeck & Ruprecht, 1982).

Siebeneck, R., 'Her First-born Son', *The Bible Today* no. 3 (December 1962), 195–200.

Sloyan, G. S., 'Conceived by the Holy Ghost, Born of the Virgin Mary', *Interpretation* 33 (1979), 81–4.

Smith, D. M., 'Luke 1:26–38', *Interpretation* 29 (1975), 411–17.

Smith, R., 'Caesar's Decree (Luke 2:1–2): Puzzle or Key?', *Currents in Theology and Mission* 7 (1980), 343–51.

Sobosan, J. G., 'Completion of Prophecy: Jesus in Lk 1:32–33', *Biblical Theology Bulletin* 4 (1974), 317–23.

Spicq, C., ' "Joseph, son mari, étant juste . . ." (Mt 1, 19)', *Revue Biblique* 71 (1964), 206–14.

Stendahl, K., 'Quis et Unde? An Analysis of Mt 1 – 2' in *Judentum – Urchristentum – Kirche. Festschrift für J. Jeremias* (ed. W. Eltester; Berlin: Verlag A. Töpelmann, 1960), pp. 94–105.

Stendahl, K., *The School of St Matthew and Its Use of the Old Testament* (Philadelphia: Fortress Press, 1968).

Stöger, A., ' "Wir sind Gottes Volk!" Bibelmeditation über Lk 1, 26–38', *Bibel und Liturgie* 50 (1977), 250–3.

Stramare, T., 'Son of Joseph from Nazareth. Problems Concerning Jesus' Infancy', *Cahiers de Joséphologie* 26 (1978), 31–71.

Strange, M., 'King Herod the Great in a Representative Role', *The Bible Today* no. 3 (December 1962), 189–93.

Swanston, H., 'The Christmas Oracle – The Imagery Behind Micah 5:1–2', *The Bible Today* no. 75 (December 1974), 189–91.

Talbert, C. H., 'The Birth of the Messiah: A Review Article', *Perspectives in Religious Studies* 5 (1978), 212–16.

Tannehill, R. C., 'The Magnificat as Poem', *Journal of Biblical Literature* 93 (1974), 263–75.

Tatum, W. B., 'The Epoch of Israel: Luke I – II and the Theological Plan of Luke-Acts', *New Testament Studies* 13 (1966–67), 184–95.

Tatum, W. B., 'Matthew 2.23 – Wordplay and Misleading Translations', *The Bible Translator* 27 (1976), 135–8.

Tatum, W. B., ' "The Origin of Jesus Messiah" (Matt 1, 1.18a). Matthew's Use of the Infancy Traditions', *Journal of Biblical Literature* 96 (1977), 523–35.

Thériault, J.-Y., 'La Règle de Trois. Une lecture sémiotique de Mt 1 – 2', *Science et Esprit* 34 (1982), 57–78.

Thorley, J., 'The Nativity Census: What Does Luke Really Say?', *Greece and Rome* 26 (1979), 81–4.

Tosato, A., 'Joseph, Being a Just Man (Mt 1:19)', *The Catholic Biblical Quarterly* 41 (1979), 547–51.

Trainor, M., 'Luke's Story of the Word', *The Bible Today* 21 (no. 1, January 1983), 34–8.

Trémel, B., 'Le signe du nouveau-né dans la mangeoire. A propos de Lc 2, 1–20' in *Mélanges Dominique Barthélémy. Études Bibliques offertes . . .* (ed. P. Casetti, O. Keel and A. Schenker; Orbis Biblicus et Orientalis 38; Göttingen: Vandenhoeck & Ruprecht, 1981), pp. 593–612.

144 *The Infancy Narratives*

Trèves, M., 'Le Magnificat et le Benedictus', *Cahiers du Cercle Ernest-Renan* 27 (no. 111, 1979), 105–10.

Tsuchiya, H., 'The History and the Fiction in the Birth Stories of Jesus – An Observation on the Thought of Luke the Evangelist', *Annual of the Japanese Biblical Institute* 1 (1975), 73–90.

Tuñi, J. O., 'La tipología Israel-Jesús en Mt 1 – 2', *Estudios Eclesiásticos* 47 (1972), 361–76.

Turner, N., 'The Relation of Luke I and II to Hebraic Sources and to the Rest of Luke-Acts', *New Testament Studies* 2 (1955–56), 100–9.

Vallauri, E., 'Natus in Bethlehem', *Laurentianum* 19 (1978), 413–41.

Vallauri, E., 'Natus in Bethlehem', *Theology Digest* 28 (1980), 39–42.

Vandevoorde, J., 'Het Kindheidsevangelie van Matteüs', *Pastor Bonus* 40 (1963), 507–15; 41 (1964), 10–14, 544–50.

Vanhoye, A., 'Structure du "Benedictus"', *New Testament Studies* 12 (1965–66), 382–9.

Via, D. O., Jr, 'Narrative World and Ethical Response: The Marvelous and Righteousness in Matthew 1 – 2', *Semeia* 12 (1978), 123–49.

Vögtle, A., 'Die Genealogie Mt 1, 2–16 und die matthäische Kindheitsgeschichte I – II', *Biblische Zeitschrift* 8 (1964), 45–58, 239–62; 9 (1965) 32–49.

Vögtle, A., 'Das Schicksal des Messiaskindes. Zur Auslegung und Theologie von Mt 2', *Bibel und Leben* 6 (1965), 246–79.

Vögtle, A., 'Die Geburt des Erlösers', *Bibel und Leben* 7 (1966), 235–42.

Vögtle, A., 'Offene Fragen zur lukanischen Geburts- und Kindheitsgeschichte', *Bibel und Leben* 11 (1970), 51–67.

Vögtle, A., 'Die matthäische Kindheitsgeschichte' in *L'Évangile selon Matthieu. Rédaction et Théologie* (ed. M. Didier; Bibliotheca Ephemeridum Theologicarum Lovaniensium 29; Gembloux; Éditions J. Duculot 1972), pp. 153–83.

Vögtle, A., *Was Weihnachten bedeutet. Meditation zu Lukas 2, 1–20* (Freiburg/Basel/Vienna: Herder, 1977).

Vogels, W., 'Le Magnificat, Marie et Israël', *Église et Théologie* 6 (1975) 279–96.

Vogt, E., '"Peace among Men of God's Good Pleasure" Lk 2:14' in *The Scrolls and the New Testament* (ed. K. Stendahl; New York: Harper & Row, 1957/London: SCM Press, 1958), pp. 114–17.

Waetjen, H. C., 'The Genealogy as the Key to the Gospel according to Matthew', *Journal of Biblical Literature* 95 (1976), 205–30.

Wansbrough, H., 'Event and Interpretation: VI. The Childhood of Jesus' *Clergy Review* 55 (1970), 112–19.

Watson, J. K., 'La naissance du dieu chrétien et la nova de l'an −5', *Cahiers du Cercle Ernest-Renan* 27 (no. 108, 1979), 2–8.

Weinert, F. D., 'The Multiple Meanings of Lk 2:49 and their Significance' *Biblical Theology Bulletin* 13 (1983), 19–22.

Wickings, H. F., 'The Nativity Stories and Docetism', *New Testament Studies* 23 (1976–77), 457–60.

Wielen, A. van der, 'De messiaanse tijd aangebroken. De boodschap van d engel aan Maria gelezen vanuit het oude testament', *Benediktijn Tijdschrift* 38 (1977), 152–7.

Wilckens, U., 'Empfangen vom Heiligen Geist, geboren aus der Jungfra Maria. Lk 1, 26–38' in *Zur Theologie der Kindheitsgeschichten* (e

R. Pesch; Munich/Zürich: Verlag Schnell & Steiner, 1981), pp. 49–73.

Willis, J. T., 'The Meaning of Isaiah 7:14 and Its Application in Matthew 1:23', *Restoration Quarterly* 21 (1978), 1–18.

Wilson, S. G., *The Gentiles and the Gentile Mission in Luke-Acts* (Society for New Testament Studies Monograph Series 23; Cambridge: University Press, 1973).

Winandy, J., 'La prophétie de Syméon (Lc II, 34–35)', *Revue Biblique* 72 (1965), 321–51.

Winter, P., 'Some Observations on the Language in the Birth and Infancy Stories of the Third Gospel', *New Testament Studies* 1 (1954–55), 111–21.

Winter, P., ' "Nazareth" and "Jerusalem" in Luke chs I and II", *New Testament Studies* 3 (1956–57), 136–42.

Winter, P., 'The Proto-Source of Luke I', *Novum Testamentum* 12 (1970), 349.

Wolff, A. M., 'Der Kaiser und das Kind. Eine Auslegung von Luk. 2, 1–20', *Texte und Kontexte* no. 12 (1981), 18–31.

Wright, A. G., *The Literary Genre Midrash* (Staten Island: Alba House, 1967).

Zakowitch, Y., 'Rahab als Mutter des Boas in der Jesus-Genealogie (Matth. I, 5)', *Novum Testamentum* 17 (1975), 1–5.

Zeller, D., 'Die Ankündigung der Geburt. Wandlungen einer Gattung' in *Zur Theologie der Kindheitsgeschichten* (ed. R. Pesch; Munich/Zürich: Verlag Schnell & Steiner, 1981), pp. 27–48.

Zinniker, F., *Probleme der sogenannten Kindheitsgeschichte bei Matthäus* (Fribourg, Switz.: Paulusverlag, 1972).

Zuckwerdt, E., '*Nazōraios* in Matth. 2, 23', *Theologische Zeitschrift* 31 (1975), 65–77.